SILENT SCREAM
True Stories of Oppression in Turkey

Mina Leyla

Edited by

Sueda Polat

Illustrated by Ummu Korku

MINA LEYLA

Born in a small town but grew up with big dreams.

Told stories as a child, wanted to be a journalist from a young age.

Always been the president of the "reading club" at school, always loved and read books, and wrote some, too.

Got upset like everybody else, made mistakes, disappointed. But got to know people who beautified her story and collected many memories.

Took interest in stories, true stories or the ones likely to happen...

Wanted to be a journalist but studied "radio and television."

Played the leading role in her story, reached her dreams, thanked God.

Began her career by putting her foot on the first rung of the ladder, worked as a reporter.

Wrote countless scenarios... worked as an editor for five years... was a source of pride for her parents.

Loved the Fall season, the flowers, the olive trees, Turkish coffee, and Istanbul...

In the battle of the oppressor and the oppressed, she took sides with the oppressed.

She couldn't love Istanbul anymore when the truth and lies were all twisted together, when friends turned into enemies, and all the holy values became just a tool of politics.

Took as a guide the verse in the Quran: "Was God's earth not wide enough for you to emigrate in it?" So, she looked at the world map.

Became an immigrant... and a refugee.

Cried some, missed a lot... but most of all, observed the people and events around her... she tried... and prayed...

Reset herself to zero...

Met other refugees, listened to their stories, and stopped feeling sorry for herself.

...and so, she has set a new goal in her life: "To be human first..."

SUEDA POLAT

Sueda Polat was born in Turkey and lived in Australia up until the age of twelve when she relocated to the United States with her family. Sueda is currently a senior student at Emory University where she is pursuing a major in Sociology and a minor in Arabic. On campus, she is a research assistant in both the history and the sociology departments, where she separately explores the topics of race and inequality, and the socialization of Muslim-American children.

Sueda has spent most of her early life working on projects about community service and human rights advocacy. In this regard, she is a member of Volunteer Emory where she is developing a service trip to help students study the topic of environmental equality. She also works on a volunteer basis with Advocates of Silenced Turkey as the coordinator for both the organization's internship program and its youth branch (Advocates of Silenced Turkey Echo). As part of these groups, Sueda works with others to tell the stories of unjustly imprisoned Turkish women within the context of Turkey's dying democracy. She has previously been a panelist at the United Nations Commission on the Status of Women to discuss women's rights violations. She is otherwise involved in her local community through various service programs and as a translator and high school mentor. Outside the field of academia, she enjoys traveling and learning new skills. Sueda hopes to pursue a law degree after graduation to better serve the cause of justice.

AST PUBLISHING

SILENT SCREAM
True Stories of Oppression in Turkey

Copyright © AST Publishing, 2021

All publication rights of this work belong to Advocates of Silenced Turkey. All rights reserved. No part of this book may be reproduced or transmitted in any form or by any means, electronic or mechanical, including photocopying, recording or by any information storage and retrieval system without permission in writing from the Advocates of Silenced Turkey.

www.silencedturkey.org

Published: September 2021
ISBN: 9798486122316

CONTENTS

About the Hizmet Movement_____9

Editor's Note_____10

Silent Scream_____13

Angels of the Aegean Sea_____56

For God's Sake, Just Shoot Me!_____111

We dedicate this work, which is based on true stories, to the thousands of people in Turkey, who have been deprived of their liberty and still face persecution. We dedicate it to the innocent people who had to flee their homeland and get separated from their families, to all victims who have set out for a new life in which they just want to live freely without further injustice, and to those who have lost all their hope of going back and living in their homeland.

We would like to thank everyone who has contributed to this book. Our sole wish is that the injustice, lawlessness, and victimization that many have been suffering from, will come to an end as soon as possible via the re-establishment of the rule of law.

ABOUT THE HIZMET MOVEMENT

Hizmet is a transnational civil society initiative that advocates for the ideals of human rights, equal opportunity, democracy, non-violence, and the emphatic acceptance of religious and cultural diversity. This widespread movement began in Turkey as a grassroots community in the 1970s in the context of social challenges being faced at the time: violent conflict among ideologically and politically driven youth, desperate economic conditions, and decades of a state-imposed ideology of discrimination that mandated a particular lifestyle.

Over the years, Hizmet has transformed from a grassroots community in Turkey to a wider global effort with participants from all walks of life. Their work is centered upon promoting philanthropy and community service, investing in education to cultivate virtuous individuals, organizing intercultural and interfaith dialogue events to promote more peaceful coexistence.

Hizmet participants are inspired by the ideas and example of Fethullah Gulen, a Muslim scholar who has expressed the belief that serving fellow humans is serving God.

For more information: www.afsv.org

EDITOR'S NOTE

Advocates of Silenced Turkey (AST) is a non-governmental organization that runs its activities on a voluntary basis since 2018. The aim of AST is to bring before international public opinion the human rights violations including torture and the unlawful court trials and proceedings, which have been encountered in Turkey especially the last ten years. After 2016, more than 160,000 innocent people lost their jobs in both public and private sectors, with accusations and unjust convictions of being connected with the coup attempt. The state of emergency, which was announced on July 20, 2016, gave the government unchecked powers - in the disguise of combatting terrorism - to persecute thousands of people with no accountability and to undermine the fundamental principles of a democratic society and the most basic principles of universal human rights and values such as freedom of expression and freedom of the press. Today, tens of thousands of highly qualified professionals such as judges, prosecutors, doctors, teachers, journalists, academics, and military officers have been detained and imprisoned in Turkey due to bogus terrorism charges. Around 5,000 of them are women, along with nearly 345 children who stay with their mothers in prisons. Hundreds of thousands of people have little or no hope of surviving the grueling atmosphere in Turkey, and as they are banned from leaving the country, they have no other choice but to flee at the risk of losing their lives by crossing the borders via dangerous routes. Some of them have not survived this difficult journey.

As the Advocates of Silenced Turkey, we engage in a number of activities in order not to keep silent about the injustices that have been taking place in Turkey where the rule of law has been suspended for a long time.

APH (Archiving the Persecution of Hizmet Movement) project of recording and archiving the testimonies of victims, aims to shed light on the injustices suffered by thousands of people in Turkey. Our volunteers have conducted hundreds of interviews and thanks to their efforts, the victimizations, and hardships that the victims experienced are now being recorded in both spoken and written formats. The main purpose of this project is to ensure that these tragic stories are not allowed to fade into oblivion but are rather recorded accurately and impartially to leave firsthand sources for future generations. We also aim to bring this persecution to the attention of academics, media organizations, human rights associations, prominent community leaders, and government representatives at the international level.

"Silent Scream: True Stories of Oppression in Turkey" is the product of a long-term endeavor. Each of our works is a compilation of real-life stories encountered by victims whose true names and event details have not been revealed for the safety of their families in Turkey. We would like to thank everyone who made tireless and valuable contributions to this work. We wish that Turkey will soon transform into a democratic society in which fundamental values like universal human rights and the rule of law are duly observed.

We sincerely thank Yasin Atik, Yasemin Atik, Fehime H. and Birgul Kocal for sharing their stories with Advocates of Silenced Turkey (AST). We would also like to thank our author Mina Leyla; book editor Sueda Polat; English translators E.Y., Reyhan Tatli, D.G.; English editors Barbara W., Hande Hur; proofreader Hande Hur; illustrators Ummu Korku, Muhsin Nazif, Asude Cekmece, Rana K, Banu Kalmaz, and everyone else who contributed to this project.

1 SILENT SCREAM

As told by

Yasin Atik and Yasemin Atik

FOREWORD

Atrocity has been staged in the world since Cain and Abel. This story is about the Turkish stage of that atrocity and about the lives destroyed after the false flag coup that happened in Turkey on July 15, 2016. It is a true story, as told by the witnesses, of a family who tried to stand out to the oppression.

After the self-staged coup in 2016, members of the Hizmet Movement, men, women, children, and elderly were persecuted, imprisoned, and exposed to widespread social lynching. People in prisons were left to death either due to the torture they were exposed to or severe diseases, and this happened while not only tens of millions of people in Turkey but also the entire world was watching. Those who tried to escape from Turkey have been tested with furious Maritsa River. So many men, women, children, and elderly have lost their lives to drowning while trying to cross the Maritsa River to achieve their freedom.

Silent Scream is a story about a family which stood up to enormous hardships, in order to be able to stay together with their children. You will burst into tears when you read how a young woman had to give birth in a janitor's small apartment without making any single sound, and what happened then to the newborn baby in the land of oppression.

SILENT SCREAM

My name is Yasin[1]... Yasin, the human being... A servant of God whose name was addressed in the Holy Quran of my Lord. After having known about the Hizmet Movement, I became even more aware of the fact that I was sent to the earth as a servant, and I was grateful for everything that was happening in my life.

I was born and raised in Istanbul; graduated from Istanbul University, Department of Philosophy, and completed my master's degree at the same university. I had the opportunity to work as a Philosophy teacher and school counselor at the private teaching institutions affiliated with the Hizmet Movement.

In 2006, my friends had introduced to me a young woman. As soon as I saw her, I knew that she was the one, my soulmate. Yasemin (Jasmine) was her name, and she was as beautiful and pure as her name. She was working in a girls' dormitory in Istanbul.

I had a good relationship with my students at school. But after I got

---

1 One of the chapters in Quran. The word Yasin, يس,, is formed by the two letters in Arabic '**Ya**' and '**Sin**'. One of the interpretations of the word Yasin is "O human being!"

married, I quit teaching and took part in a business association, which was established within the Hizmet Movement. I had a good dialogue with the people I had met during the time I had worked at that association.

Although I never had asked for it, I somehow ended up at the business association's forefront and established friendly relations with some bureaucrats in the government. The scope of these relationships was limited entirely to open dialogue and had nothing to do with obtaining anything illegal in the name of the Hizmet Movement, whatsoever.

In June 2008, our son Enes joined us, and our daughter Reyhan was born after another two years. That year was also the year we moved to Edirne. It was 2015 when our home rejoiced with the birth of our daughter Nalan. We were enjoying happy days as a family; however, things were not going well for the Hizmet Movement members, in general. I was in charge of the General Secretariat of the Business Association in Edirne. Since the government corruption scandal[2] in December 2013, hence long time before the false-flag coup in 2016, Hizmet Movement was under constant pressure. Police operations were conducted in the name of fight against the so-called Parallel State Structure[3], innocent people were being

---

[2] The December 17-25, 2013, corruption scandal in Turkey refers to a criminal investigation that involves several key people in the Turkish government. Prosecutors accused 14 people, including several family members of the cabinet ministers, Suleyman Aslan, the director of state-owned bank (Halk Bank) and Turkish-Iranian businessman Reza Zarrab, of bribery, corruption, fraud, money laundering and gold smuggling. In March 2016, Reza Zarrab was arrested in Miami. In November 2017, Zarrab cooperated with federal prosecutors and has become key witness in the case of money laundering and violating sanctions on Iran.

[3] The 'Parallel State Structure' is a term invented by Turkish president Tayyip Erdogan following the major corruption scandal related to him and his family members, to refer to followers of the Hizmet movement, particularly within the government bureaucracy.

the subjects of crime files and they were being announced as culprits, without due process of law. Believe it or not, we would find out later that even the informers who were to speak against the Hizmet movement members had already been determined one year before the coup. Who were those informers? One of them was the city's greatest trustee (!), a businessman who made frequent donations to the Hizmet Movement, entirely voluntarily. In short, we were blacklisted, everything about us were being recorded; addresses, phone numbers, car plates, and such. They were pretty much saying: "Why did you throw a monkey wrench into our business?" Otherwise, all of their accusations were untrue and unsupported by facts.

Even the people with whom we were on good terms, or the ones who we thought knew us very well, were now turning their faces away from us. I was worried more for my wife and children than for myself. I was often warning Yasemin about not going anywhere alone, and not eating anything in the places she didn't know well.

It was 2016, the year of immense hardships. One of our friends was arrested in the middle of the night after his house was raided by fifteen police officers, just because he had criticized the president of the country on Facebook. Every now and then, we were noticing some strangers around the building where we were living... they were watching us.

...

It was months before July 15 when I got a phone call from Yasemin on my way to Istanbul for a business meeting. Our apartment had been raided by police! After showing the search warrant, eight police officers had searched everywhere for hours, under the witness of the building superintendent and two other neighbors. I don't know what they were looking for or hoping to find. They probably didn't know, either. I had no criminal record, neither anybody I knew had a police record. Their sole intention was to intimidate us, to disturb our peaceful family life. On their way out, they wrote and signed a document stating that "No criminal elements found in the apartment." We later found out that the houses of fifty more people from the Hizmet Movement had been raided on that same day in the city... the houses of the school principals, directors of the civil society organizations, etc.

If you live in a small city and the police raided your house, everyone hears about it, and even if you're innocent, you can't easily break the prejudice against you. There was constant pressure on us; occasionally we were getting insulted. It was impossible to leave peacefully in that city anymore, so we moved out from there, even changed our cell phone numbers.

Well, the situation was not so different in the city we moved into. We couldn't see it at that time, but the roads to that self-staged coup were already being paved, brick by brick. In that small city we were now living, there was a private school of the Hizmet Movement and a business association where I was working as the general secretary. After a while, the members of the boards of the school and the business association began to send us their notarized resignation letters. We couldn't figure out what was going on. We would later learn that the members of the business association had received visits from some MIT[4] personnel and they were threatened.

In May 2016, we had moved to Istanbul. Barely a month later, the police raided our new place again on May 29. Although I had no official duties at the time, they had an arrest warrant for me. On that day, I was in Germany to follow the International Turkish Olympics[5] which was organized by the Hizmet Movement. I learned from Yasemin that those who came to our house were pretty rude. They had searched every square inch of the house, from the exterior parts of the windows to the kitchen cabinets. I have to admit that I had a brief hesitation about returning to Turkey, but then I said, "So be it." and came back. My family, my children were there, and it was my homeland.

...

I came back to Turkey, but I never went home; I could not. The police could make another raid anytime. That is how my 25-month-long saga of hardships began, which was a time period in which my endurance and patience were really tested. I could not stay at home, but the government could issue an arrest warrant also for Yasemin for some ridiculous reasons. I'm talking about June of 2016, one month before that coup attempt of July 15. The government had already begun to take people from their homes and interrogate them on the basis of false and fabricated allegations.

---

4 The National Intelligence Organization (*Turkish: Millî İstihbarat Teşkilatı*, MİT)
5 Since 2016, it is known as "The International Festival of Language & Culture (IFLC)", with the mission of showcasing global youth talent in the performing arts to celebrate our world's cultural diversity and create opportunities for international friendship-building around shared human values. For more information, please see https://intflc.org/

Before long, the July 15 false flag coup attempt would be staged so that nobody would speak out against all those government operations which were conducted, violating the rule of law. We didn't know about that "coup de theatre" then.

THAT AWFUL DAY...

On the day of the coup attempt, I was staying in an apartment that I was living with a couple of friends... there was an arrest warrant on them, too. I had also rented another apartment for my family to stay in. It was close by, so we could see each other frequently.

On the evening of July 15, 2016, my wife and children were in my place. We were watching a movie together, and I didn't want to look at the messages I was getting to my cell phone, in order not to interrupt the magic of the moment. It was around 11:00 p.m. that I learned about what was going on and called my brother in panic. We were thinking similarly: "What a shame! Looks like they will pass the buck to us!"

I couldn't sleep until morning that night. Yasemin and the children were also scared -- they did not want to go to their place that night. I later learned that the next morning, when they went to their place, they were so nervous that they entered their apartment building quietly, using the back door. An immediate and vast witch hunt had already been launched on the morning of July 16. I didn't want them to stay alone in their apartment any longer. They stayed either with me or at my sister's place.

Nothing changed for the better in my country on the following days. Blamed for the attempted coup, the police had a much more valid excuse now to arrest us. It was unclear how long this would all continue.

I was looking for ways to stay all together with my family. We couldn't stay in one-bedroom apartments because those kinds of places were usually used for prostitution, and police were making raids on those places frequently. We were finally able to rent a very small place in the basement of an apartment building. I used one of my relatives' name to sign the lease contract.

We could take at most a third of our furniture and belongings to that small new place. Being so afraid of getting caught by the police, we had left our old apartment before even the moving truck arrived. A couple of relatives ended up moving our belongings. Our new place was in a relatively less expensive neighborhood, it was also hosting people coming from different backgrounds. It was ideal for us, people around would not pay any attention. I told some of our new neighbors that I was working for a factory which was well known in Turkey.

Those days were so difficult to handle. We didn't leave that small apartment unless we absolutely had to, and when we did, we walked around so nervously, afraid of getting caught. We couldn't use a credit card, and we couldn't take care of any business matter which required us to show our ID's. It was September now, and two of my kids were going to school. We were dropping off them to school and then picking them up, but God only knows what we were going through. Police were carrying out major and wide-ranging checks frequently and giving those operations names such as "Wolf Trap". Thousands of police officers were participating in those operations, and criminal record checks were carried out for 30,000 - 40,000 people a day. You didn't need to enter a government building to undergo a police check, even if you were in a park pushing your child on a swing, police would come and ask for identification. Whether you were traveling in a city bus, or driving your own car, or simply sitting on a bench at seaside didn't matter, you could be asked to show your ID wherever you were and whatever you were doing. A lot of our friends had ended up being caught like this. We had to use different methods to avoid the police when taking the kids to school and back home.

A mass shooting incident was carried out in the Reina nightclub in Istanbul on New Year's Eve of 2017. Soon after, the information was spread that the terrorists who carried out the attack were hiding in the neighborhood we lived. So, the police presence and patrols increased even more. Dropping off the kids to school and then picking them up became very complicated and risky. There were police officers everywhere and we had to walk around them to reach the school.

One day when we were about to take the kids to school, there was some disturbance right in front of our apartment building. Apparently, it was a gunfight, and someone was shot. We got so scared and left our apartment immediately just in case police would knock on our door and ask us to bear witness for the incident that happened. Another day, right when my son went out to the street in front of the building, I saw someone with a mask on his face setting up kind of a barricade to clash with the police. Immediately, I grabbed my son and took him in with fear and panic. Although we were accused of being terrorists, these were definitely not the things we were familiar with.

TOUGH DAYS...

We were trying to fit into the 500-square-foot apartment in the basement of a building with three children. Of course, as the saying goes, a body would fit into any place where a heart fits. Actually, it wasn't the apartment that was too small for us, it was the circle of oppression around us, and it was getting tighter.

We could not tell anyone about our true identity. I was a teacher, but I couldn't even say that, as if being a teacher was a crime. We were trying to keep our distance from people to a certain extent and not having any guests into our place. When we were taking the kids to school, we were cautioning them every day, "Don't tell anyone which school you have been before! Don't tell anyone your home address! Don't say anything about us!"

While we were coming from the school with children, I was doing everything to avoid any police checkpoint. Meanwhile I was trying my children not to notice anything. One of those days, my son told me, "I know you're escaping from the police!" At that time, a friend of mine was with us who was a police officer but recently had been dismissed from his job by a decree-law[6]. I said, "No my dear, my friend here is a police officer, too. Why should we run away from them, anyhow?" But God knew I was running away. I was scared and was trying to keep my family together.

Both Yasemin's parents and my parents offered to take care of the

---

6 In the aftermath of the coup attempt, around 150,000 public officials have been dismissed from their jobs by decree laws of the government, and without due process of law.

children, they said that they could bring them to school and then back home every day. But we didn't want to do that. We wanted to spend all of our days together with our children because we didn't know for how long more we could do that. We could be caught by the police any day, imprisoned and even killed there. We were all together in this, and our worst fear was being apart from each other.

...

In December, I found out that an investigation had been launched against Yasemin, too. She was being investigated because she had worked in a charity foundation which was helping needy people. Several of her friends who had been arrested had sent word to my wife to be cautious, saying that the police had asked them frequently about her.

Then something happened that we didn't expect – my wife Yasemin was pregnant again! We said, "Whatever is from God is most welcome" and made a plan. We would go to a hospital right before the delivery and tell them that we came here from another city, and we would leave the hospital right after the baby was born.

But when we heard that a close friend of Yasemin was taken into custody as soon as she stepped foot in a hospital for giving birth, we knew we had to change our plans. During her entire pregnancy, Yasemin was able to see a doctor only a few times. The delivery time was approaching, we were desperately trying to find a way out of this dilemma. Was there a way out?

I was spending my days trying to find a solution. During the daytime,

I went to several hospitals, just to sit around and observe the patient admission procedures. Do they always ask for identification from patients? Was the social security number absolutely required? Would it be all right if we had entered from the emergency department entrance and said that we forgot our IDs at home? Could we use the fire stairs to run away in case we had to? I even went through the floor plans of a couple of hospitals. But we were so far away from any kind of illegality all through our lives that I could not visualize us doing anything unlawful.

While we were trying to find remedies for this problem, another situation came up. The nose of my eldest son, who had brain surgery when he was five months old, was bleeding every now and then. We were terrified, but we couldn't go to see a doctor because of the fear of getting arrested. I had never felt so desperate in my life. I was continuously thinking about these two problems. After some time, I decided to take my son to the hospital using my nephew's ID and managed him to have an MRI exam. Thank God, it was not something important.

Until now, I've talked about what my family and I went through during this time period. But our brothers and sisters in the Hizmet Movement have suffered immense tragedies, too, especially in the first 6 months after the so-called coup attempt on July 15th. So many people were arrested without any legal justification, beaten, and tortured. The victims of persecution were forced to leave their homes, and their families torn apart…

…

The baby's due was getting closer and closer. What would we do? We thought perhaps giving birth at home could be an option. After all, there were many women giving birth at home. We looked into it. Apparently, even if you were to give birth at home, you had to register the baby immediately to the system in order to receive any kind of help later. I set up a Facebook account using a fake name, to look for a midwife to help deliver the baby. I was looking for someone who was dismissed from her job by decree-law because only someone who was a victim herself could understand our situation and help us. But during that time period, nobody was trusting anybody else. I had found a couple of nurses who had lost their jobs, but we couldn't reach them later on as the due date approached. We finally found an old midwife. "Okay, I'll help," she said. But what if something goes wrong? What if the baby dies? And what is worse, what if something happens to Yasemin? The more I was thinking about all these, the more nervous and upset I was getting. I was so helpless, so desperate. When I finally accepted that pretty much nothing was under my control, I decided to put my trust in God, and God alone.

Yasemin was doing her own preparation and research. She was watching videos about giving birth at home, coming up with strategies based on her previous experience, and most importantly trying to stay calm. It was not just about giving birth at home. She was supposed to give birth and not to make any sound in that tiny apartment. We simply couldn't trust anyone! Giving birth and not making any sound at all! Can you imagine that? Even the thought of it was making me so nervous.

...

It was around midnight of September 10 when Yasemin told me that the baby was to come that night. I have to admit that I was at my wits' end. And not just me. Everyone in our family was so nervous! We immediately called my brother-in-law because he was going to pick up the midwife from her home.

The delivery process began around midnight and ended around 9:00 a.m. in the morning. My soulmate, Yasemin, the love of my life, would turn into a true hero in my eyes after that night. A man normally loves his wife but that night my respect for Yasemin has multiplied several times over. She was such a strong woman and she had not made a single sound during the entire night, like a sheep giving birth in pure silence.

Please allow me to let my wife Yasemin tell you about that night. Because whatever I write will be insufficient to describe that night, my words will be incomplete and shallow.

GIVING BIRTH AT HOME

It was the first month of 2017 when we found out that we were going to have a baby. I wish I could tell you things like "We were so happy that we were walking on air." but that was not what we felt upon learning about our pregnancy. The idea of giving birth to a baby at such a stressful time, and in the midst of financial difficulties, was not very charming. The arrest of women right after they had given birth was not a common practice yet, or maybe it was but we didn't know it. Towards the end of my pregnancy, a friend of mine was taken into custody at the hospital right after she gave birth to her baby. We heard similar stories soon after and got really frightened. Another friend of mine, who was also arrested right after the delivery, sent me a word with her mother -- she strongly cautioned me against going to the hospital. Apparently, police had asked her several questions about my whereabouts. But what were we supposed to do?

Earlier, one of my friends had suggested, "Would you consider giving birth at home?" I didn't lean towards it at first, but things were pretty much unfolding in that way. We contacted several midwives, but no one was willing to help. We couldn't trust everyone, either. Finally, we were able to find an old midwife who agreed to help.

I never saw the midwife before the birth, we talked only over the phone. I had no idea about what kind of things I would need, I had never given birth at home after all! The midwife told me to get a large tarp, a big trash can, and garbage bags. She would bring the rest.

We were the kind of people who were scared to death every time the doorbell rang or when we heard the sirens of a passing police car. I went into a store thinking: "Why would a heavily pregnant woman buy a large tarp?" The storekeeper asked me, "Are you going to wash a carpet on it?" I had to lie, so I said, "Yes, sure, washing the carpet!"

Our apartment was very small and there was no soundproofing in the walls, insomuch as you were to sneeze, the neighbor was able to hear you. Three little children in that tiny apartment, together with a man and a woman who had completely put their trust in God. On September 10, it was around midnight when I understood that baby was to come soon. When I let Yasin know about it, he got so excited and stressed. He put his clothes on and started pacing in the hallway, but that made me even more nervous.

My severe contractions had started at midnight, and they kept going on until the midwife arrived at 6:00 a.m. She had also brought another friend along. Meanwhile, I had read the chapters, Maryam and Taha, from Quran, which gave me spiritual support.

We were in a fifty-square-foot room, and the midwives were getting prepared for the birth. They laid a quilt on the floor and the tarp on the quilt. They had told me to pace around the room, apparently, that was supposed to help. Was I scared? Of course, I was! But I was more afraid about the baby rather than myself.

YOU CAN'T YELL!

"You will give birth, but you must not scream; you cannot make a single sound." We would probably think that it was a joke if anyone had said this in normal times. But then again, we were far away from normal times. So, when the midwives told me, "You shouldn't yell." I only said, "Yes, I know."

Later, people asked me about this so many times, "How did you manage to give birth without yelling?" I only had one answer: "Because it had to be like that." Because if I screamed, all the struggles we had for months to be together as a family could have been wasted, my home could have fallen apart. And because… I knew that I was not the only woman doing this. Dozens of my dear sisters, everywhere in the country, were in the same situation as me. They had given birth under similar conditions without making a sound. And I knew that my Lord would give me strength, as He gave strength to them.

If you're a mother, you have to think about your children before yourself. That night, I was as worried for my children as I was for my baby. We could have overcome all these difficulties somehow, but I wanted my children not to see my misery. I didn't want to leave such an image in their pure minds.

Thankfully, my Lord did not embarrass us in any way that night. On Monday, September 11, at 9:12 a.m., our baby was born: Yusuf. Yes, we named him after Joseph, all the Josephs in the dungeons. After my previous births, I could not even open my eyes out of exhaustion, but this time my Lord gave me so much strength. Our baby looked so beautiful and healthy. Thank God!

All that stress we'd been under for weeks was finally over. I was not arrested. The baby was healthy; I was doing fine. When the midwives left the room and Yasin came in, we couldn't even speak. He lay down next to me; we looked at each other and started crying. All that stress and fear would wash away only with tears. For half an hour, we cried nonstop…

…

Then my little daughter Nalan woke up and came to the room. She was surprised to see the baby and ran to the other room to wake up her brother and sister: "Wake up, wake up! The baby is here!" All praise be to my Lord, Who did not embarrass us!

…

SILENT SCREAM

Illustrated by Asude Cekmece

A BABY WITH NO ID IN THE LAND OF OPPRESSION!

I had become a father for the fourth time. All of our other children were born in a hospital, so we had not paid too much attention to all those tests and vaccines a baby normally would have in the first 24 hours. After the birth, the midwife put a piece of paper in my hand and said, "Get these from a pharmacy." I didn't know what they were about, but the pharmacist understood immediately and asked, "A newborn baby?" I gave short answers quickly and got the items on the list. I never went there again, we were trying not to go to any store a second time, just to be on the safe side.

When I got home from the pharmacy, I was on tenterhooks until the midwives had finished their job and brought me into the room. I stepped into the room being so afraid of seeing something terrible; I have to confess that I didn't even care too much about the baby at that time; I was worried about Yasemin's condition. I breathed a sigh of relief when I saw that she was fine. I laid down next to her and we cried and cried.

Normally people get so happy when they take their newborn baby into their arms for the first time. We got happy because we got not caught by the police. All our efforts, hopes, and prayers were for this. In that land of oppression, we were trying to protect our family and avoid the destitution that our children could face if were arrested.

The following days passed under a different kind of stress. We drove half of Istanbul for a simple vaccine, to find a doctor to examine our baby without asking for a birth certificate. We also needed to get an ID for Yusuf, our innocent baby who was born in the land of oppression. We couldn't get done most of the things. When we went to hospitals or private clinics, they were first asking: "Where's his birth certificate? What's his social security number?" When confronted with such questions, we were finding an excuse and simply getting out.

When babies are born, their height, weight, head circumference, etc. are measured at regular time intervals. But we couldn't take Yusuf to a doctor, so we couldn't get him measured. I bought a digital kitchen scale and a tape measure, and we started measuring him every day.

We again thought of changing our apartment because more and more people knew us now in the neighborhood, and they wanted to come to visit the baby. Besides, it was getting really difficult for six people to fit into that tiny apartment. It was extremely stressful to be at that tiny place with four children. Cleaning, cooking, all the noise that the kids were making… it all meant stress. We couldn't afford an internet connection, so once in a while and then I was going to internet cafes to download some cartoon movies and bring them home on a flash drive. We were watching those cartoons to keep them busy.

Some families around helped us financially. We had already minimized our spending. I had bought a large sack of flour, and we were cooking different things with it as much as we could.

Did we ever rebel against God? Never! We had friends who were arrested, and they were facing life sentence for the crimes they did not commit. We were grateful that we were still together, at least for now.

There was an arrest warrant on me, and Yasemin was taking the kids to school. But it was only a few months later that we found out that police made a raid at our old address to arrest her, too. I told Yasemin, "If one of us were to get caught, it should be me…so that you can take care of the children." And I started taking the kids to school.

We never thought about giving ourselves up. We were innocent, and we weren't going to surrender to the tyrants. Of course, there were times when I was feeling so weak, when I thought, "I can't take this anymore, let me just surrender." But soon after my Lord gave me strength and patience.

POLICE CAME TO OUR PLACE!

About four months after Yusuf joined our family, we moved to a new apartment. The reason was increased police presence and patrols in our neighborhood. This time we preferred, as a precaution, a residential compound with many high-rise buildings in it. Our apartment was on the eleventh floor of a building.

One night the doorbell of our apartment rang for a long time. When I looked down out the window, I saw several police cars in front of the building. The children were asleep, I told my wife to take the baby and go up to the roof using the fire stairs. I didn't want her to get caught together with me so that she could take care of the children. Meanwhile, the doorbell was ringing again. I pushed the intercom button to unlock the building door and waited, like a lamb to the slaughter. I said to myself: "I had a good time with my children, but this is it! It is over now! Now what remains for me is to be hopeful and remain patient."

I waited and waited… for seconds actually, but they seemed like hours to me. Nobody came up the stairs, or took the elevator to our floor. I looked down out the window again and saw the police officers taking some other people away. Was I glad to see that? Well, I was pleased, but I was also sorry because maybe they were taking away some of our brothers from the Hizmet movement. Probably they had children, too, and had hopes for a better future, but it was all over for them.

After I made sure the police officers were gone, I went up to the roof. My wife Yasemin was sitting on the floor, hugging the baby and sobbing. These were the kind of fears they let us live.

…

It was the month of Ramadan[7] and we invited my parents to dinner. While my wife was cooking in the kitchen and I was outside, our baby fell off the table and hit his head on the floor. When my parents came, Yusuf was crying nonstop and throwing up; his eyes were not lining up, either. We were so desperate. Meanwhile, the sun had set, and it was time to break the fast, but no one even touched the food. My father who is not an emotional person, was sitting at the edge of his seat and shedding tears.

A few hours had passed, but there was no improvement in Yusuf's condition, so I took my chances and brought him to a doctor, using my nephew's ID card. They took a CT scan and ran some other tests.

---

7 Ramadan is the ninth month of the Islamic calendar, observed by Muslims worldwide as a month of fasting, prayer, reflection and community.

Thankfully, there was no injury from the fall. That was a tough day for us, and it was that day of Ramadan when I made the decision that we should leave Turkey. We couldn't stay there any longer. But I was also very worried. I didn't care about myself; but how could I forgive myself if something were to happen to one of my children?

With each passing day, the conditions were becoming more difficult and as a result, the thought of leaving Turkey was gaining flesh and bone. One day, when the kids wanted to spend some time in a nearby playground, we went out. But when we saw the police officers in the park asking the people for their I.D.'s, we turned around and went back home. Yasemin and I were adults, we could stay in our apartment for a long time, but it was so painful for us to know that we had to keep our children indoors most of the time. That was totally unfair to them and, of course, very difficult for us to explain to them.

I was inventing games so that the kids wouldn't feel the stress of this gloomy period too much. One day I purchased a large map of Turkey and hung it on the wall. We studied the cities one by one and dreamed together. We talked about the famous sights in each city, what to eat, where to stay, etc. It was as if we were traveling in our minds. I promised them that we would go on a tour after the schools were closed.

But when the summer arrived, of course, we couldn't go. I didn't want to be a liar in the eyes of my children, so I said to them, "OK, we can't have a tour of Turkey, but guess what? Maybe we can tour Europe." God willing...

It was nice to dream with the kids, but there were facts, cold hard facts. Yasemin and I were talking more and more to each other about the possibility that we could get caught in front of our kids. We had to leave Turkey as soon as possible. It was June 2018. We finally made a definitive decision; we were to leave in July.

Illustrated by Ummu Korku

ROADS OF MIGRATION

We didn't know how to contact smugglers. We called one of our friends who had left Turkey after the July 15 coup attempt and got a phone number from him to contact the smugglers. Of course, there were many risks involved to consider. Yasemin and I talked about all possible scenarios for hours. After all, we were people who believed in divine destiny. We had to seek refuge in God... and just as we took a risk at birth, we had to risk our lives now in order to be able to live free. Yasemin proposed to get life jackets, but I didn't think we needed them, so I just bought arm floaties for the kids. To tell the truth, I was thinking that I would just hold on to Yasemin in case of an emergency. She was our hero. There was an arrest warrant on both of us, with the charges of being a member of terrorist organization (!). So, she was my wife, my partner in life, and in cause. She was also my partner in those alleged crimes we had never committed. She was my greatest support, my eternal love!

For two years, we hadn't revealed our home addresses to anyone except some close family members. We did the same thing again... didn't tell anyone else that we were leaving. And we repeatedly warned our close relatives to not tell anything to anyone about our plans. That was pretty much the new norm after July 15, nobody was trusting anyone. You couldn't know who would tell on you to the police.

...

We had definitely decided to leave, but that bitter feeling of departing from our loved ones was so intense. Neither my family nor my wife's family opposed it, on the contrary, they encouraged us to do so. "You must leave this place," they said. We didn't say goodbye to our families all at once. They came to our place in small groups and on different days. Each time, everyone was bursting into tears, although they wanted us to leave the country. It wasn't easy to leave all your loved ones behind. We were very sad, too, but they had left us no other choice.

I remember that last day when my mother-in-law was at our home.

My wife and her mother cried for so long without even saying anything. Finally, they both said, "There is nothing else to do... this must be done, and we have to endure it." I remember them hugging each other and crying even more.

...

It was a hot day in July, our hearts were fluttering with excitement. We prayed for a long time before we left home. Our close friends were driving ahead to warn us about any police checkpoint. After a while, they called us to tell that there was a police search ahead, so we took the next exit to a rest area. We eventually arrived in Edirne[8] earlier than we planned, so we had to wait. Our friends didn't leave us alone. We spent some time in the mall around, had dinner, but we were very nervous. In order not to attract any unnecessary attention, we even split up into two groups.

...

When the day turned into night, it felt like time went faster. From the moment on we came in contact with the smugglers, we moved incredibly fast. After driving some times in a car together with smugglers, we then walked for a while. It was so dark, soon after we met up with two other families waiting in an open field. Yasemin and I were both carrying a backpack. Our baby was in Yasemin's arms, and I had my youngest daughter on my shoulders. I was also holding the hands of our other two children.

---

8 Edirne is a Turkish city at the border with Greece. Part of the Maritsa river flows in Edirne and forms the border between Turkey and Greece. It is a natural barrier on the border and has become a major route for migrants from a variety of countries attempting to enter Europe.

We were a total of six adults and seven children, following the two smugglers in the middle of the night, with constant prayers on our tongues, and our hearts fluttering like a pigeon's heart. It was pitch black and we were told not to use any kind of flashlight. I had no idea where we were going. We could only feel what kind of land we were walking on, sometimes it felt soft, and sometimes it was rocky. We were hearing motor vehicle noises and dogs barking in the distance. How close were they to us? We did not know. It was as if an animal or someone would come out from the bushes any moment.

We were walking under the dim light of the moon when I suddenly slipped and got stuck in the mud. I managed to pull out my foot only with the help of my friends, but my waist was hurting so much (Even to this day, it still hurts from time to time). After a while, my daughter's shoe got stuck in the mud. I first intended to leave it there in order not to fall behind the group. But I quickly changed my mind and began searching for her shoe, digging the mud with my hands. I found it after a couple of minutes. I didn't know then how important that shoe would be later.

We slid down a steep hill slowly, sitting on our pants, and reached the riverbank. I don't know why, but we had to walk along the river for another half an hour, then we waited quietly in the reeds. Soon, a small boat came by, and we got on it. Everyone was so silent while we were crossing the river, even our ten-month-old baby didn't make a single sound as if he had felt it. It lasted 45 minutes. Along the way, I whispered to the ears of my children, "We are almost there, don't be afraid. I am so proud of you!"

...

It was July 3, 2018, when we had left Turkey, where in last two years we were being falsely accused without any evidence as being terrorists and being hounded. It was the first hours of July 4 when we first stepped on the land of Greece, with our high hopes for a new life. A cautious relief had replaced the tense silence within the group after crossing the Maritsa River. Everyone was talking in a much more relaxed way.

The place where the smugglers left us on the Greek side was not very promising, to be honest. We were glad that we had safely crossed the river, but the tough journey was far from being over. This place was not any different from the Turkish side, swamps and dense bushes everywhere. The thin branches around were pricking like a needle and ripping our clothes until we finally reached an open field. Since we had no idea where we were, we turned on our phones and checked our location. Yes, we were in Greece, but there was another river lying in front of us. We had to find a way to cross it, but how?

Smugglers actually had said that some people would come and get us. We called and asked again. "They'll be there!" they answered. Upon hearing that we decided to wait there and rest. Of course, we did not know what kind of dangers were awaiting us in the middle of that dark night. The women sat down on the ground wrapping their arms around the children while the men stood around, being on the lookout for any kind of trouble.

We waited like this for quite a time, but there was no one coming to get us. We were calling the smugglers frequently and asking questions like

"Where are they? Do they know where we are?" Finally, they told us "They won't be able to pick you up, so you better start walking. Walk straight ahead."

We set off again and followed a trail in the woods. While walking, mosquitoes were attacking and biting us ferociously. I wouldn't be exaggerating if I said a hundred mosquitoes attacked every one of us. Although we wrapped the children in blankets to protect them, even they were bitten many times.

The smugglers told us to go to the north, but we did not know which direction was north. We opened Google Map, but it was of no use. We walked with the kids for six hours. That was so hard to do; everyone was exhausted. We ended up at another bank of the river, and at that point, we decided to call the police.

Police had first sent a fishing boat towards us which was close by. The fisherman on the boat pointed with his finger to the police that was coming towards us and tried to make a joke: "Erdogan is coming to get you!" I guess he thought that was funny.

The police officers took us ashore, carrying us in two groups. That's when we found out that we had crossed the Maritsa River in three stages.

Illustrated by Ummu Korku

REFUGEE, BUT FREE AT LAST

We were taken into a detention center. All of our bags were emptied and searched. Also, they let us remove our clothes and did a partial strip search. We were all shocked to be exposed to that. Maybe it was routine, but it was so offending, especially being treated like this in front of our children. And then, covered in mud from head to toe, we were put in a detention room. The children were so tired they fell asleep. Yasemin and I washed our clothes and shoes in the bathroom. Then we prayed. We were both exhausted, starving, and very thirsty. We hadn't thought of taking water with us earlier. When we had asked the smugglers over the phone, "Where can we get water?" they had answered, "If you find a puddle, drink from it."

We had never told our kids the real reason of this "road trip." When they woke up in that detention room, it was the first time I had talked to my kids about what has been going on recently in Turkey: "The president of our country was jealous of our accomplishments and ordered for our arrest. But we didn't want to leave you, so we are on this journey…" Our little daughter Nalan and baby Yusuf were of course too young to understand anything, but the two older children cried and asked, "Will we not see our friends again?" I told them, "You'll make new and beautiful friends here. A whole new world is waiting for you to be discovered."

…

It was about 9:00 a.m. when we were taken into the detention center. Fortunately, we were the only ones in the detention center, and we were as comfortable as we could be, given the conditions. But because we were not checked in during the night, no meal was ordered for us, and we were starving. After a few hours, the police officers brought a few loaves of bread and cheese which was enough for all of us. We said, "Alhamdulillah." (All Praise be to our Lord) for He had not let us to be forgotten, even here.

The walls of the detention room were full of words that the refugees had carved in their own languages. In one corner, I saw "Allah var, gam yok" written in Turkish (God is here, so do not grieve!) It felt so good to see it, like seeing a dear friend. In another corner, I saw another writing:

"Yumurcak TV" (which was a children's TV channel in Turkey). I said to the kids, "Guess what? We have even Yumurcak TV here! Let's watch!" They came running, and we all laughed together.

...

If you keep any person in a room for consecutive three days, he'd be severely depressed. We knew this very well of course, from firsthand experience because of all those things we had lived through in the last two years. But the detention center was extremely tough to handle. It was a small room; the baby was in our arms all the time, the conditions were really difficult. We wanted to get out as soon as possible but we were not allowed to. We even thought that maybe it would have been better if we had never started this adventure. They weren't mistreating us, but it was really tough to spend three days with four children in that small room.

...

After two long nights we spent in the detention center, they transferred us to a refugee camp on the morning of the third day. That day, until evening we waited in the heat for them to finalize where we were to stay in the camp. It was again very difficult to soothe the children. They didn't want to take a nap, either... time was just not passing.

Around 6:00 p.m. in the evening, we were told that our places were ready. On that day, a total of nine Turkish families were taken to the camp, and they put us all in the same section of the camp, Section C. Three families were staying in each container, but we did not complain at all. It was definitely much better than that small room in the detention center.

They usually brought us meatballs for meal, but we couldn't eat them because we thought they were not halal (kosher), and gave them to the cats and dogs hanging around the camp. One of the women in charge of the camp was surprised to see this and asked, "We prepare these meals for you; why don't you eat them?" We did not have enough English to tell her the real reason, and we didn't want to be rude, so we just said, "We're vegetarian." The next day a surprise was waiting for us. They had fixed some eggs and home fries for breakfast! They were so kind.

True Stories of Oppression in Turkey

Source: AST International Human Rights Art Contest

"Why do you stay in prison, when the door is so wide open?"

Rumi

TIME TO DEPART

After a few days in the camp, we were allowed to leave. We took a ten-hour-long bus ride to Athens, and we decided to stay there until we could figure out what to do next.

We were free at last! No longer did we have to worry, "Would the police raid our house tonight? Will we get separated from our children? Will we be imprisoned and if so, for how long?" We didn't have problems like that anymore, but our hardships were not over. We had spent all our savings in the last two years since we were not allowed to work in Turkey by government decree. We were running out of money very fast because everything was more expensive in Greece due to Euro.

We decided to move to some other countries in Europe because there weren't many job opportunities in Greece. We went to the airport several times to try, but we were not allowed to travel. Yusuf didn't even have a proper ID, let alone a passport; and none of us had a Schengen visa which was required for foreigners to travel in Europe.

We decided to move to Thessaloniki in northern Greece because it was less expensive to live there than in Athens. Maybe we could find a job there. I was thinking, "Even if I can't get a job, I can go fishing and sell what I catch, and if I can't sell the fish, then we'll eat it, so at least we will have food." I could raise chickens in the backyard, and we would eat their eggs. Somehow I thought it would be easier to live there.

We rented an affordable house, enrolled the kids in a school, and tried to hold on to life, but financial difficulties surfaced on a regular basis. I had a U.S. visa, and I asked my wife several times, "I can go ahead and set up a new life for us in America, and then you'll come later?" But she refused, saying, "What am I going to do here with four kids on my own?"

But after four and a half months, she told me, "Yes, you need to go." She had realized that there was no future for us in Greece.

...

I've been in the United States for two and a half years now. I kept hoping for a better future, with a terrible longing in my heart, being away from my family. After 13 long months apart from my wife and children, I started to breathe again in November 2019. We reunited as a family here in the United States.

Yes, it was very difficult to stay in Turkey, but being away from my homeland is hard, too… missing so many people. I talk to my father on the phone frequently. We say to each other that we are fine. But God knows how much I miss him and how much I want to hug him again. Just like I wanted to hug my crying children when we were apart, when they were saying on the phone, "I miss you, daddy… I miss you so much."

I have never blamed the Hizmet movement for any persecution, hardship, or trial I have experienced. I am sure of my innocence, and I am sure of the innocence of Fethullah Gulen[9] and my brothers and sisters who have been slandered as terrorists. I have never witnessed Fethullah Gulen saying anything which could incite any form of terrorism. Hizmet is my way of life, and I don't regret anything I've ever done on this way.

Now, I live a very simple life and work in a job that is totally unrelated with my profession. I have not forgotten my brothers and sisters in Turkey. I pray for them all the time and even share some of my earnings with them. I do not complain about anything I have experienced, but I will complain about those who have put us through this horrible ordeal. I pray to my Lord to call them to account on the Day of Judgement, on behalf of all the oppressed people.

---

9 Fethullah Gulen is an Islamic scholar, preacher and social advocate, whose decades-long commitment to education, altruistic community service, and interfaith harmony has inspired millions in Turkey and around the world. Described as one of the world's most important Muslim figures, Gulen has reinterpreted aspects of Islamic tradition to meet the needs of contemporary Muslims. He has dedicated his life to interfaith and intercultural dialogue, community service and providing access to quality education. For more information, please visit www.afsv.org

2 ANGELS OF THE AEGEAN SEA

As told by

Fehime F.

FOREWORD

This book is about a heavy drama which is based on true events that took place in Turkey under the Erdogan government, where, since many years ago, it has been the law of rulers that is in force and not the rule of law. You will read in tears how a young couple in love with each other were announced to be terrorists in just one night, although they had not even hurt an ant in their lives. You will witness how they struggled to survive together with their two tiny babies, and how they have decided to flee their home country where there was no right to life for them anymore. But all their efforts went in vain and led to a terrible tragedy when their boat sank in the Aegean Sea.

We do very much wish that what you are about to read in this book was nothing but a scenario, a fiction. But unfortunately, each and every sentence in it is true. And it was our responsibility to pass on the screams that we have witnessed, the screams of the women and their babies when they fell off the sinking boat into the dark sea in the middle of a dark night. When all the reasons and hopes had ceased to exist, there was only One Authority to take refuge in, the Almighty God.

On that night, the Aegean Sea has become the grave of many innocent lives. One woman, even though she didn't know how to swim, has survived. But unfortunately, it was in her destiny to witness the last minutes of her husband and her two tiny babies that she was holding in her arms. Immediately after such a traumatic loss she has experienced, she found herself in the courtroom where she was held accountable for the crimes she had not committed. The conscience of humanity was silent!

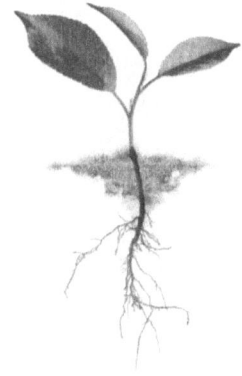

My only hope is that one day we can live happily again, together as a nation.

A BEAUTIFUL MOVEMENT AND A BEAUTIFUL SOUL

I was the youngest in a family with two kids; a little girl who loved her father and was his little princess. My journey in Hizmet began during my middle school years thanks to my older brother. I still remember the selflessness of my sisters in Hizmet who, without any complaint and with pleasure, would mentor and guide us even during their final exams in college. The fruits of these pure actions eventually manifested in my decision to become a college guidance counselor although my college degree was in physics. I chose this path in order to help others the way my mentors helped me and to pay my debt of goodness forward. I was young and idealistic. Just like any other girl, I also had my own dreams.

When my close friends first introduced me to the man that was soon to become my husband, I somehow immediately understood that he was my soulmate. But there was a problem; my father, who was very protective over me, would not allow me to marry someone who was not from our hometown.

One day I told my future husband: "My family would not allow us to marry each other but if you were to remain strong and patient, I would be willing to fight for this marriage." Without even thinking he accepted and then he kept his promise.

When my father heard that he was not from our hometown, he expressed his much-anticipated disapproval. But I was going to keep my promise, too. I was going to find the right time to convince my father to meet him.

My father, who once said 'never,' was quite impressed when he had met my husband and had seen his good heart. He had approved our marriage, saying, "What more could I want from God than a son-in-law like him?"

MY PARADISE ON EARTH

They say that "If you have a spouse and a job that you love, you live the Paradise on earth." I had definitely found my very own Paradise on earth. God had blessed me with a job and a husband whom I loved. My husband was a teacher and he was in love with teaching. His students were his lifeline and source of happiness. As an educator myself, I understood his feelings very well. As a family, we were quite happy and trying to do our best to be beneficial to people around us.

Shortly after we got married, I found out that I was pregnant. When my dear son was born, I felt that the missing piece in our family portrait was complete, and that beautiful days were waiting for us in the future. This feeling only lasted until my paradise on earth slowly began shattering around me.

My husband was teaching at one of the schools that were affiliated with the Hizmet movement. The rising tension between the government and the movement was causing great worry and uncertainty for the future. The school administrators told my husband and other teachers to apply for positions in other institutions and find different jobs because the school was in danger of being shut down by the government at any moment.

Upon their warnings, my husband applied to prestigious schools in Ankara and Istanbul and was soon met with offers from some of them. Unlike many other teachers, my husband had an additional certificate in teaching the mind and logic games and thus he had some advantage in the job market. We had to make a decision soon and accept the offer of one of the schools.

While we were busy with all these, we didn't know that a dark nightmare was soon upon us: the staged coup attempt of the July 15th, 2016. Neither did we anticipate that all the schools that gave a job offer to my husband would soon slam their doors in our faces.

THE BLOODY SCENARIO STAGED

One summer evening, we were drinking tea on our balcony. We had just arrived back from our trip that we made to see our parents and relatives in our hometowns. Our baby was sound asleep, and we were sitting in a peaceful silence. Since we did not own a television, we received the news by a late-night phone call. It was my father, anxiously telling us that there was news everywhere about a coup taking place in Turkey that night. With great worry and fear setting in, we followed the news through Twitter until late in the night. Our home was in a relatively secluded area, so we did not witness the mass of people pouring into the streets that night. However, based on the president's speech that night, it was clear that our life was about to get significantly harder to bear.

As the days progressed, the schools that my husband and I were working were both shut down by the government so we helplessly looked for some jobs. There was a deafening silence from the schools that were once eager to hire my husband. We couldn't find any job and were drowning in our rent, bills, and childcare expenses. We had no choice but to abandon our home and live with my parents together in their house. My husband's job search continued but to no avail.

After a while, we went to my husband's hometown and stayed there for around a month. Around this time, we found out that my older brother who was living in Ankara had also lost his job. He suggested that we go to Ankara, where we could stay at his house and where there were more job opportunities because it was a big city. We would go and stay in his place for a year. We were hopeful that we could find a job in the big city with many opportunities and make our own living and not be a burden on others.

I cannot count how many jobs my husband had applied to. To some extent we could understand why his academic applications were getting denied; there was a witch hunt going on in the education sector, after all. What was so disappointing was that he could not even get a simple waitress job. The reason was that he used to work as a teacher in one of the Hizmet schools before. When the job interviewers would hear that, they were immediately ending the conversation. Some of the restaurant owners even told him, "If I were to hire you, they would close my place down."

It was such a frustrating and depressive situation, especially for my husband. He began to question everything: "What did I do wrong? Why am I labeled as a terrorist when I wouldn't even harm a fly?!"

He even tried to do jobs like painting or computer programming, but nothing worked. None of his pursuits bore any fruit. It was as if all doors were slammed in our faces and close friends were turning their backs on us. Our life, once a paradise, became a living hell. I am grateful that we at least had our families to rely on during these dark times, but they were not wealthy people, living off pension income alone.

PREGNANT AGAIN

How could a woman be sad upon hearing that she's pregnant? That was, unfortunately, the case for me; I was simply devastated. We were struggling financially, we had no hope in the near future, and worst of all, pregnant women who were affiliated with the Hizmet movement were getting arrested after they gave birth in hospitals. I became deeply depressed as I took all of these factors into consideration. There was no arrest warrant on us, yet, but our close friends were getting arrested and sent to jail, one by one. So many innocent people were being tortured, ripped apart from their children and families, or even killed. I felt guilty and fearful for being pregnant at a time like this; I was constantly crying in desperation. If it hadn't been for my loving and supportive husband, I do not know how I would have endured those dark days. May God bless him.

It had been exactly one year since that devastating day in July which darkened our lives. Since we were unable to support ourselves financially, we left Ankara and went to my parents' house. The plan was to stay there for a few days and then to go to the town where my husband's parents were living, settle down there, and try to find jobs. The next morning, as we were sitting around the breakfast table, my mother-in-law called to tell us that the police had raided their house and were looking to arrest my husband.

Upon hearing that we changed our plan and stayed in my parents' hometown. We rented a small apartment and tried our best to make it a home for ourselves. However, both my husband and I were emotionally and mentally so drained that we began to take out our anger on each other. Thank God that we couldn't stay angry at each other for long; our love would always triumph above our hardships.

My husband had managed to find a way to provide for his family which didn't require him to interact with others: fishing. He was hoping to catch a lot and sell it to others to make some money. However, due to his lack of experience, he could only catch just enough to feed our family. Nevertheless, we remained grateful.

Soon after, I gave birth to my second child. My husband was, unfortunately, unable to accompany me in the hospital because there was an arrest warrant on him. During the delivery, I had lost an excessive amount of blood and from the look of the doctor's face, I could tell that something wasn't right.

After the baby was born, I didn't hear the normal cries of newborn babies. Shortly after I would learn that my baby was taken to the intensive care unit because she had swallowed a large amount of sac fluid. Meanwhile, my mother who was waiting anxiously outside of the delivery room was notified of the possibility that both her daughter and newborn granddaughter could die. She could do nothing but helplessly sob for hours.

GOD, PLEASE DON'T LET MY BABY DIE!

We stayed at the hospital for a long time. The days were dragging painfully slowly as I was unable to see my baby, who was in intensive care. I felt like I was going crazy by the minute. No one was giving me any clear answers. I was unable to even get out of bed because I had gone through surgery. I couldn't take it anymore; in between loud sobs, I begged the doctors to talk to me, to say something about the situation of my baby. At last, one of the doctors responded and gave me an explanation; he said that my baby had an issue with her breathing which meant that I couldn't nurse her. There was nothing I could do but wait; my baby could continue to live or die any day.

I had to be patient and pray to God. While other pregnant women had their husbands by their side, my husband couldn't share these moments with me. I felt completely and utterly alone. I waited and waited as each painful minute ticked by. One morning, I was notified that I would be discharged from the hospital. However, my baby was to stay in the hospital.

It had not been half an hour after I came home when we received a phone call from the hospital. We were told to immediately return because the baby had to be transferred to a research hospital.

My knees gave way and I dropped to the floor, sobbing uncontrollably and thinking that my baby was going to die. Just twenty days ago we had lost my aunt's husband to a surgery that took place at a research hospital. A man who strode into hospital on two feet came out in a coffin.

My husband panicked and told me, "I want to come with you no matter what may happen!" But I could not allow this. I didn't know what was going to happen to my baby, and if he also got arrested, I would not be able to survive. I told him that I couldn't handle losing him.

I was about to face the reality of the situation. The professor who was working at the public hospital had transferred five babies, including mine, into the research hospital's ICU. However, we were not given any explanation and were kept in the dark throughout the process. We got more and more frustrated due to the lack of communication. They admitted me to the hospital again and allowed me to nurse her once every three hours. Those were probably the times when I faced the most severe psychological and physical distress, and that my dear husband couldn't be there with me was making everything much worse. Ten days later, we were finally discharged and allowed to go home.

Illustrated by Ummu Korku

Our desperation was a clear signal that
there was no right to life for us in this country…
our only hope was to take refuge in a country
where we could be free.

STRUGGLE UPON STRUGGLE

Out of fear of getting arrested, my husband was not stepping foot out of the house. It was my responsibility to take the kids to the hospital for their vaccination shots when needed.

During this time, my husband's best friend was fired from his job. His wife was my close friend and under the immense pressure of financial troubles, fear and worry for the future, and piling struggles she had lost her meant health. While she was undergoing psychological therapy, she became diagnosed with cancer and died a short time later. My husband was devastated since he could not be there for his friend during his difficult times.

It seemed like one bad thing was happening after another. We felt our patience slowly wither as things seemed like they would never get better. Our country had turned into a prison, and we felt like prisoners in our own home.

We could not have stayed in our parents' houses because of the risk of getting arrested. We were labeled as terrorists by the government and public, and we had lost our trust in everyone as people were being rewarded for informing people like us to police. Our desperation was a clear signal that there was no right to life for us in this country…our only hope was to take refuge in a country where we could be free. Of course, this was not an easy decision to make but we had no future here, no hope. It was all dark around and we were waiting in vain for this darkness to end.

Our families wouldn't approve us to leave the country, besides we didn't have the money for it, anyway. But we had to leave, at least we had to try it. How could we continue to live here with the fear of getting arrested any day? In a country where there was no rule of law, no freedom! We had to leave.

With the blessing and help of my husband's family, we started our journey. I was worried about my family's reaction but when I told them we were leaving, thank God they didn't oppose and said with teary eyes: "Yes, you should go." They knew that the very thing we were afraid of would catch up to us if we continued to stay here. Meanwhile, my older brother had gotten arrested just a short time ago. The government had prepared an indictment and charged my brother with using a communication app called ByLock[10]. He never used that app, but it didn't matter. They first dismissed him from his job by a government decree and then arrested him. 25 days after they released him, they arrested him again. My parents were so shattered with all these, so they gave us their blessing to flee the country, even if with heavy hearts.

---

10 ByLock is a smartphone application that allowed users to communicate via a private connection. It was launched in 2014 on Google Play and Apple App Store, it was permanently shut down in March 2016. Turkish authorities claim that ByLock is exclusively used by members of the Hizmet movement to ensure the privacy of their conversations. Users of ByLock were considered as terrorists in Turkish courts.

OUR DEPARTURE

In the midst of making decisions, talking to our families, getting into contact with those who smuggle people across the border, two months had already passed. I wouldn't be lying if I told you that I spent that entire two months crying. If I were going alone, or if it were just me and my husband, it would not be a problem. But we had a two-and-a-half-year-old and an eight-month-old with us and therefore things were becoming much more complicated and frightening.

For people like us who had never broken the law in their lives before, it was a very unsettling feeling. I was lost in my own thoughts, contemplating whether we were doing the right thing or not. We could potentially die while trying to cross the border illegally. When I told this to my husband, he responded with, "Don't even think about death, we have to do this."

Whenever I would lose all my hope, he always encouraged and comforted me. During that time, an arrest warrant was issued on my name as well and I couldn't leave the house anymore in order not to take any risk. It seemed like all signs were pointing to our decision to leave the country. It was either that or imprisonment and being stripped away from our children. My husband and I were so attached to each other that we would rather walk into the unknown together and not stay away from each other or from our children.

The sun was about to set, and I took one last look at my country.

ANOTHER DARK JULY

July…I guess it was my destiny to live through two dark, painful days of July in different years and I had no other choice but to play my predestined role. One was July 15th, 2016, the day of the so-called coup; and the other, two years later, was the 28th of July 2018.

My husband spent so much time and effort to come up with the safest plan to cross the border. He was in contact with the human smugglers, so I was only aware of the fact that we were to leave on the 28th of July.

The separation from our families felt like death. The lump in our throats would swell and our eyes would fill with tears every day at the thought of leaving our loved ones. My dear mother had lost eight kilograms in just a week due to depression. She was crying every single day. My father was so attached to my son, he never let us see him cry but I had no doubt that he was shedding his tears into his heart. However, he told us many times, "Leave and gain your freedom, at least save the future of your children."

While we left in broken pieces and tears, we were very sad but not afraid. There was only the fear of getting caught and arrested, and not the fear of the difficulties that awaited us on the road.

It was around 6:30 p.m. in the evening and we were sitting at a cafe, drinking tea. That was our meeting spot with the smugglers. I felt like I was in one of those mafia movies. A few men with many tattoos came soon and put us in a black-tinted car. We were driving along the roads that we had never seen before, and our fate was in the hands of complete strangers.

...

The sun was about to set, and I took one last look at my country. We were in the middle of an olive tree field standing alongside three other families whom we didn't know. One of the smugglers was constantly assuring us by saying, "There's nothing to be afraid of. Look, you see that place across the sea? That is where you will go. You will ride on a luxury yacht and arrive at freedom in just twenty-five minutes!" His words were very convincing and reassuring and gave us a peace of mind, for at least a little while.

My husband was carrying our son and I was carrying our daughter with baby carriers. Once two more families joined us, we walked towards the nearby shore for a few minutes.

It was pitch black around us, we were unable to see whether it was indeed a luxury yacht that was awaiting us. I learned later the hard way that it was actually a small boat. In order to avoid questions, the smugglers were deliberately creating an air of alarm and hurry. I got on the boat first and was seated next to the captain because I had a baby with me. I was so terrified that I kept whispering to my husband, "Please don't leave my side."

A total of sixteen people were packed on a boat with a maximum capacity of four. You may ask how in the world we accepted to go through with this, but we were being rushed, threatened, and pushed. We thought they were doing all these with the fear of getting caught. What choice did we have? We asked for life jackets, and we were told, "You'll find them on the boat, now hurry, we can't waste time!"

For the first time in my life, I saw despair and surrender in his eyes.

WHEN REASONS CEASED TO EXIST...

We had just departed, and our eyes were glittering with hope and enthusiasm. The sea waves were strong, and the air was cold. Splashes of ice-cold water were shooting our faces like daggers, and we were trying to protect our babies with our hands (There were three babies on board).

It had been only ten minutes when we heard the scream of a man sitting at the very end of the boat; the boat was springing a leak! The already fearful passengers went into a state of panic, while the captain remained calm. He told us not to worry and that it was normal for some water to leak in when the engine is running! We needed to feel safe and secure, but we were confronted with the cold truth when we insisted on wearing the life jackets. There were no life jackets on board except for one, which was likely for the captain.

We were completely helpless. The kids were drenched in water and were shrieking and crying in fear. While no one else made a sound, the terror was written all over their faces. Water was still leaking into the boat, prompting the captain to stop the engine and head to the back of the boat. After a minute or so, those terrifying, heart-dropping words made their way out of his mouth, "We are going to sink!" Nobody was silent anymore, every passenger began screaming and crying all at once. The captain frantically made his way to the front of the boat and tried to restart the engine, but it wouldn't work. He began cursing himself, questioning why he made the decision to turn off the engine. That one mistake was about to cost us our lives. We were yelling out, "God! Dear God!" while the boat was slowly sinking, and we were trying to hang onto the side of the boat that was still above water. It felt like we were witnessing the apocalypse with the pitch-black night around us. The children were crying and wiping their faces every time they would sink and surface again above the water. We were trying to hold onto the sinking boat, jumping off every time when a large wave hit, and crying and begging to God constantly. The captain most likely took the only life vest and escaped the chaos. We were so occupied with trying to stay alive that we had no time to figure out where on earth he went.

Meanwhile, we tried our phones, but no one had service. At last, someone's continuous attempts worked out and we immediately dialed 156 for Gendarmerie. When they finally answered, we began screaming, "Our boat sunk, we will all die here! Please help us!" They asked us for our location, but at that time we were trying to hold onto the sinking boat, and with poor phone service there was no way we could send our location. "We can't do it, please track us from the phone signals," we implored, "If you don't come soon, we will all die here!" "Send your location!" said the voice again… "Send your location!"

What happened then? The rest of the boat sank slowly, the phone line went dead, and we helplessly shrieked as the sea continued dragging us around. It was truly a life-or-death situation, the cold big waves separated wives from their husbands, and children from their parents. As if it were the judgment day, everyone was struggling for his own life and couldn't help anyone else. Then I saw the members of one of the other families that we were sharing the boat with, the mother was being dragged out with her child, while the father was pulled away in the opposite direction by the waves.

The waves were ripping people apart from each other, but we managed to stay together. We held each other tightly, our son and daughter still in the baby carriers. I was terrified and sobbing uncontrollably, asked my husband, "What are we going to do now?!" Like always, my dear husband remained optimistic and assured me that everything was going to be alright. He was a good swimmer, so he told me, "Hold onto me, I'm going to swim towards the coast."

He was hopeful and determined. I don't know for how long he swam like that, pulling his entire family on his back. And then, all of a sudden, he stopped, he couldn't go any further. For the first time in my life, I saw despair and surrender in his eyes. My dear children could not even make any sound anymore due to fear and cold. While I didn't want to accept it, it seemed like the journey we embarked with such hope was coming to an end. I knew what was about to happen, though I would have given anything to prevent it.

With my heart torn into pieces, I looked at him and we said our last goodbyes to each other. He was a wonderful husband to me and a loving father to his children. With exhausted eyes, he looked at me one last time and quietly said, "I'm tired." These were his last words. In the realm of reasons, it was tiredness. In the Divine plan, it was the predestined time of death. If it had been up to him, he would have never given up and left us there all by ourselves. As soon as he said these last words, I immediately grabbed my son as my husband let himself go into the dark water. Only a few seconds later he came back up to the surface. I could neither think nor do something. My husband would soon disappear in the dark and cold water again, but this time he would not come back alive. I was now all by myself, holding my son with one hand and my daughter with the other.

Oh God, You illuminate the night! Oh God,
You let light shine out of darkness!
Please take me to the shore of safety!

PROPHET JONAH INSIDE THE WHALE...
ME IN THE MIDDLE OF THE SEA!

It was pitch black, I was in the middle of pounding waves, with my two children in my arms. All the reasons had ceased to exist. I felt like Prophet Jonah, completely alone. I needed a "Savior" Who would have power over the sea, over the darkness, over all the reasons.

While my husband was an excellent swimmer, I was not good at swimming despite having grown up in a coastal city. I constantly kicked my legs to stay above the water and cried for help. As a woman who had given birth twice, I don't think I yelled during the deliveries of my babies as much as I did in those moments. I could hear the voice of another survivor far away in the darkness. When I was tired of yelling, he would yell, and when he was tired, I would take over... We hoped that someone would hear our cries, but there was nobody else around.

There was no way we could survive; I knew that I would sooner or later get tired of kicking my legs. My dear son had probably swallowed a lot of water when he went down and resurfaced with his father. When I was using the last bits of energy I had, I saw my son's little head slowly tilt to the side. It was only a few minutes later that I witnessed my daughter give her last breath. That night, following their father, my two children left this dark, ruthless world and made their way to Heaven as angels, where they deserved to be...

One would expect that, a woman who witnessed her husband and two children die one after another right in front of her eyes, would either lose her mind or let herself sink into the dark waters to join them. I don't know what I felt. I had lost my sense of feelings and got completely numb... no thoughts, no reaction. The only thing that came to my mind was, "If I let go of my kids, they will never be found anymore; if we're going to die, at least let our bodies be together."

I sunk and resurfaced on the water countless times, still holding my dead children. I was crying and begging to God as saltwater entered through my nose and my mouth, burning my throat and lungs, "Oh God, You illuminate the night! Oh God, You let light shine out of darkness! Please take me to the shore of safety!"

...

Seconds seemed like hours, I was constantly kicking my legs in the water to stay afloat, and this had caused excruciating pain in my back. I was exhausted, about to give up. I wanted to take off my shoes to remove some weight, but I couldn't as I was still holding my children's lifeless bodies. At that moment, I saw a coast guard boat passing by. I screamed at the top of my lungs, "Heeelp! I'm right here! Please help meee!" They were so close, but weirdly they just passed by without even looking in our direction. I was hearing the loud cries of the other survivor nearby, but the boat didn't stop for him, either. Did they ignore us on purpose? Did they leave us to die there? God knows...

JONAH'S PRAYER

"There is no god except You; exalted are You.
Indeed, I have been of the wrongdoers."

(Quran, Chapter Anbiyâ, verse 87)

I continued to kick my legs with my last ouncse of strength left. Meanwhile, my husband's dead body resurfaced and began floating in the water. He was trailing right behind us as if he didn't want to leave us alone. This gave me strength; yes, he had departed from this world, but he became an angel and accompanied us in our darkest hour.

A little later, a fisher boat saw us and quickly approached. A man immediately threw down a ladder and asked me, "Are you alright?!" I nodded my head. "How about your kids?" I could only say, "I lost them!" and extended my children to him. The man suddenly started sobbing uncontrollably. But I did not have time for this; I had to reach for my husband's body and take him inside the boat. When I quickly turned around and tried to approach his body, I heard a loud cry in the darkness; "Please, save meee!" It was a young girl, only sixteen years old... In the spring of her life, while her peers were enjoying life and having fun, this poor girl had accompanied her parents on this journey of hope to escape the oppression and persecution. Alas! She was now in the middle of the pitch-black sea by herself. When I heard her cries, I hesitated for a very short time. If I were to leave my husband, I could never find him again. But what was at stake was the life of a young girl. So it was obvious what to do, I saved the girl. Meanwhile, the fisherman found and saved the other man who was crying out for help. I don't know how it happened, but the captain of our ship suddenly appeared and got on the boat. In a moment of deep anger, the surviving man attacked the captain, while I was simply numb. With empty eyes, I kneeled beside my children's lifeless bodies and watched them helplessly. I was neither crying nor embracing them. I just stared at them... just stared.

WE'RE SAVED

A while later, the coast guard boat came once again. They performed CPR on my children, telling me that they were still alive as they transferred them in another boat to an ambulance waiting near the shore. But I knew my babies had already become angels…

The fisherman handed us over to the other coast guard boat. They obviously didn't care about our health and safety because we spent another half an hour looking for other lost people. It never occurred to them to transfer us to another boat and take us to the shore.

When we finally made it to the shore, I realized that I had lost my hearing ability in my ears; I tried to decipher what people were saying by reading their lips. My throat and stomach were burning so much from swallowing seawater that I couldn't even drink the freshwater they offered me. We begged the authorities with tears in our eyes to contact our families and tell them about what happened. They didn't care about our requests. They treated us as if we were stricken with plague.

"YOU ARE A MURDERER! YOU KILLED YOUR OWN CHILDREN!"

We were waiting desperately on the shore, completely drenched and struggling to breathe due to the seawater we swallowed. I couldn't stop crying and constantly recited, "God, why didn't you take me too? I have no one left!"

At one point, when I was going to wash my face, I saw my father and my sister-in-law. Apparently, they were not allowed to come next to me, so they were waiting far away on the shore. With tears filling my eyes, I cried out, "Daaad! They're all gone!" As I said that, I heard my sister-in-law shriek, "My brother!" and then she collapsed on the ground. My dear father, not knowing how to react, kneeled down beside her and kept looking at me.

...

A while later, a man who lost his wife and his little child approached me and said that the bodies were kept in the ambulance, and in order to see my children, I had to insist on asking the police. In a situation like this, the only thing that could possibly connect two complete strangers, like myself and this man, whose paths might never have crossed otherwise, was destiny. My request to go near my children was denied. I felt as if we were a bunch of objects in a display case while the news reporters were taking our pictures. I'm sure that several catchy headlines were running through their heads as they took the pictures of the poor people suffering in front of them. As a matter of fact, later we would see those inhumane and heartless headlines such as "The boat carrying Hizmet terrorists has sunk, several deaths!"

At last, the van that they were waiting for arrived and we were taken to a nearby hospital by police. I was sitting next to the sixteen-year-old girl that I had saved. On the way, I sobbed the entire time: "I lost my everything! Everything! Why am I even living? Why didn't God take my life?!" That poor girl had her father, aunt, and two cousins on the boat. Her aunt was drowned when the boat was capsized. I have later learned that her mother was already in prison. That young girl had experienced so much pain in her short lifetime and turned into a mature adult early on, like thousands of other children who were the victims of this evil time period.

When we got to the hospital, they didn't immediately take us in but rather they let us wait in the van and it felt really like a torture. We then understood the reason. The news reporters were to take pictures but the heroic police officers didn't have their special jackets on them writing "Counter-Terror" with big letters. They wanted to wear those impressive jackets and pose for the cameras next to the dangerous terrorists (!) like us. So we waited. Finally, their jackets were brought, they put them on, and took us inside the building, not all of us at once, but one by one in order to give more opportunities to the reporters to take good pictures. As for our deep pain and health? No one could care less.

I no longer had any purpose or hope left in life, so it wouldn't be true if I told you that I was upset because of all these ridiculous acting. When I was taken to the doctor, I was injected with a sedative and felt utterly numb for hours, unable to cry, only capable of looking around with lifeless eyes. I continued to beg for my children, "Please take me to them!"

After a while, they took me to the morgue. While waiting there, I saw the bodies of two women being carried in black body bags. We were in the same boat only a few hours ago. The ones who died had finally saved themselves, they had escaped injustice and oppression, whereas the ones like me were left behind, all alone with our harsh problems. Staying alive felt like kind of punishment.

While waiting in front of the morgue in my wet clothes and shoes, being in deep sorrow and grief, I felt so vulnerable and desperate. I was only able to exchange a few somber glances with my father looking at me from upstairs. I wanted nothing but to run into my father's arms and hear him tell me that everything was going to be alright, but that was impossible. They were not letting us to do that.

Suddenly, the female police officer who was standing next to me began to yell, "Stop crying! You are a murderer, you killed your own children! You should have just stayed at home with your kids! What the hell were you doing on that boat?" I was in utter shock. Before I could respond, the man who had lost his wife and child came close by and politely told the officer, "Ma'am, you can never understand us. Do you know what it means to be fired from your job for no reason and then to have to work in horrible jobs for seventeen months just to bring some bread to your family? Have you ever experienced the pain of not being able to take your child to the park for months in order not to get arrested although you have not committed any crime? Have you left us any other choice but to leave this country? How can you criticize us?" Despite his grief, he had never lost his manners. The police officer was not understanding a thing, and she continued to blame and berate us. Another officer who was standing in the back made a facial expression to signal us to pay no attention to what the female officer was telling us. This is exactly what we did.

Oh Lord, what a long night that was! May God never let any other mother have to speak to her dead children in a morgue. My daughter and son were lying on a stretcher together. I hugged, kissed, and caressed their cold bodies. I closed my son's mouth which was open from swallowing so much water. I knew that they couldn't hear me, but I kept asking, "Why did you leave me, my babies? Why?"

It was 2:00 a.m. in the morning when we were taken outside the building to wait for my husband's corpse to be brought. But then they told me that they were going to take me to the police headquarters. "What about my husband?" I implored, "I don't want to leave without seeing him!" They said: "We are still looking for him in the sea, we will bring you back here when we find him." I didn't have the chance to object.

I was still wearing the same wet clothes, and all the other survivors were in the same situation. Due to the shock and panic of the moment, it hadn't occurred to my mother to bring me a change of clothes, but thank God, she had an extra shawl and tunic top for herself, and they allowed her to deliver them to me. When we arrived at the police headquarters, I was not allowed to change my clothes in privacy. "Look," I told them, "I have nothing on me other than my wallet, you can take that too if you want to, but please don't humiliate me like this!" They didn't care, so I had no choice but to change my clothes in front of the female officer.

The officer who accompanied me was the same female officer who berated me in front of the morgue; she continued to insult and incite me saying things like, "How could you do this to your children?!" So many things were happening so fast I didn't even bother to reply. She must have been so surprised at how patient I was that she felt the need to ask me, "Did they give you kind of a medicine or something, why are you not responding?"

Meanwhile, I continued to ask for my husband so many times. They believed that he had escaped by swimming to the other side of the shore, although I repeatedly told them, "He died right before my eyes." I had lost my sense of time so I couldn't tell how long it had been. I was able to overhear a police officer in the next room talking over the phone and saying that my husband had been found. Then I heard the female police officer responding, "Let's not tell her, she already lost both of her kids, she is crying nonstop."

A few minutes later they came and asked me, "Are you hopeful about your husband?" I told them the same things I had been telling them for hours, "He died right in front of my eyes, he can't be alive. Please take me to the hospital to see him one last time." They didn't care.

GOD, WHY DIDN'T YOU TAKE MY LIFE TOO?!

All of these events occurred on a single night, a dark Saturday night in July. In the morning I would be taken into interrogation and have my fingerprints taken. I would like to mention here that during the interrogation I was at least respected for the pain I was going through, and no one mistreated me. Everyone was giving me pitiful glances. The police was asking questions like, "Who were the human smugglers? How did you get into contact with them? Give us their names and descriptions." I told them that I didn't know, and I truly didn't. My husband was the one who was in contact with them.

I was still crying uncontrollably. Finally, on the condition that we keep it quiet, they said that they would let me see my parents. I cannot describe to you how difficult it was to bite my lips until they bled and force my tears back into my eyes when all I wanted to do was scream and cry my heart out. I so much needed my family, especially my mother. I tamed the storms that raged in me and ran into her loving arms. We embraced each other for minutes, weeping silently. As for my dear father, he seemed to have aged many years within a single night. "Dad! Daddy!", I cried, "Why didn't God take my life, too? How can I stand this pain?" It was one of those moments where a father felt completely helpless in comforting his child. "Don't say that sweetheart," he said with a shaky voice, "God spared you for us!" Then my mother saw the wet shoes on my feet and immediately took off her slippers to put them on me. She did not care that she was barefoot. The sixteen-year-old girl whose name I do not wish to give, unfortunately had to spend an entire day in wet clothes while being taken from place to place. Her mother was in prison, her father was newly arrested, and she had to wait for one of her relatives to bring her a change of clothes.

...

I spent that entire Sunday going to the bathroom every hour. My breasts were in immense pain because I couldn't nurse my baby, so I was hand expressing the milk over the bathroom sink. Meanwhile, I was frequently being taken into the interrogation room. When I was told that I was to spend the night in custody, I felt like I was truly going to lose my mind. To be put in a cell with many strangers and criminals after going through so much pain and suffering was unbearable to me. I cried and begged them not to send me there and that I would sit obediently in the corner on a small chair. "I promise I won't cry or make a sound! You won't even notice my presence!" but to no avail.

Because there was no space in the other detention cells, they decided to put me in a storage room instead. I was all alone in a dark room. Every time I closed my eyes, I would relive my husband and children's final moments, and felt like I was going to die. No matter how much I begged them not to leave me alone in the room, nobody paid any attention.

In that pitch-black room, I sat on a blanket, cried, and prayed the entire night. I was unable to cope with the stinging, burning pain in my heart. In between my sobs, I opened my hands and said, "God, what did I do wrong?! What did my husband and my angel babies do wrong to deserve all these? My husband had not even hurt a fly in his life!" I cried so much that I lost track of time, and finally managed to fall asleep towards the morning. I frequently woke up, hoping every single time that it was all just a nightmare, and my loved ones were next to me. I was in a mental state that I was actually waiting for a miracle to happen. Despite witnessing my husband and my children lose their lives in front of my eyes, I would hope that they somehow would come back. It felt so real; it was like they were not going to leave me. I was constantly looking at the window, or the door...

In the morning the night officer's shift had ended and before he left, he updated the newly arrived officer with my case. I don't know why, but the new officer was so hostile towards me. I had not even said a single word when he began yelling at me, "You are going to address me as officer, I am an officer!" Then he left but came back after half an hour. I had sat on a wooden chair the entire night. He must have not been able to find anything else to say as he ordered, "You can't sit there. Come in front of the iron bars and sit on the floor. The camera will record you better here." I didn't have any energy to argue with him, so I followed his order. He would check up on me every half hour and find a ridiculous excuse to shout at me. In the meantime, another police officer came and asked me if I was hungry. "No," I said, "I am not hungry."

BROUGHT TO COURT

With the appointed public defender next to me, I waited sitting on a bench in the courthouse to be called in by the prosecutor. Across from me were my older brother, mother, and father looking so sad and anxious. The public defender was like a doomsayer, constantly talking about the worst scenarios, "They are definitely going to arrest you, don't forget to ask for permission to attend the funeral of your husband and children." I was already going through a deep trauma and was becoming more afraid of the idea of staying alone in a cell. I felt more and more stressed out and as if they could do anything, I began begging my brother and father, "Please do something. I lost my husband and two children, don't leave me alone!"

My dear father was devastated and began praying through tears, "God! If You wish, please take my life right now, but please don't let them take my daughter to jail!" My brother couldn't bear it any longer and said to the lawyer, "What kind of heartless people are you?!" to which the lawyer coldly replied, "I have years of experience, I know what is going to happen…"

Shortly after, the prosecutor called us in. I can't say that I have seen mistreatment from him. He asked me to explain everything. As I was telling them what I went through in complete honesty, I have noticed the court reporter weeping as she typed. I was also in tears; "I want to attend the funeral of my loved ones." I begged the prosecutor. He replied saying that they will consider my request.

Later, we went downstairs and appeared before the judge. I cannot remember much about what happened in the court. I just could not stop crying anymore. I remember hearing only a few words; "Travel ban, judicial control, going to the police department weekly for signature." My lawyer added, "My client is going through a deep trauma, we request the minimum sentence for her."

As soon as we left the courthouse, which was around Monday afternoon, we headed to my husband's hometown, which was around 500 miles away from Bursa. Our phones would not stop ringing as our friends and relatives were calling to say their condolences. The only thing on my mind was whether my husband and children were brought from the hospital in Bursa to my husband's hometown. On the way, I found out the news on the internet that the municipality of Bursa had denied to provide funeral transportation services, on the grounds that my husband and my babies were terrorists(!) My husband was one of the most kind-hearted people I have ever known and my babies were only in diapers. Upon learning all that, my grief became even more difficult to bear. But then again, I found consolation in thinking that God did not want us to receive any benefit from their blood-stained hands.

WHAT HAPPENED IN BURSA?

While I was dealing with detention, interrogation, and court, the person who was really going through all the stress was my poor sister-in-law. She had rushed to the hospital upon hearing what had happened and then she had to perform one of the most painful things in the world, identifying her brother's, niece's, and nephew's corpses. She then traveled to Bursa in order to arrange a funeral vehicle and agreed to meet with the driver of the vehicle at 9:30 p.m. in the evening in front of the forensic medicine building.

While she was dealing with all these, her parents were still unaware of their son's death. She then called her uncle in their hometown to give him the sad news and told him to bring her parents to Bursa without telling them what had happened. Up until they came to Bursa, my parents-in-law had thought that their son was arrested and in custody. In fact, they spent their entire journey praying for their son to be released soon.

When they arrived in Bursa, my poor mother-in-law had seen several other relatives who had come all the way from Istanbul, and she said: "My son is going to be so happy when he sees us all here." It was then when my sister-in-law gathered up all of her courage and looked into her mother's eyes and smiled, "Mom, stay strong and try to smile because my brother joined to God's Eternal Mercy!" I found out later that my mother-in-law had collapsed to the ground in devastation, and my father-in-law had stood there, frozen, for minutes.

At 9:30 p.m., my sister-in-law called the driver of the funeral vehicle but couldn't reach him. She called some other people in charge, an official working in forensic medicine and an administrator in Bursa municipality. They both told her they will not give a funeral vehicle for my husband and babies, under any circumstances. When this news got public attention on Twitter, the mayor of Bursa was responding by saying, "They are Hizmet terrorists, nothing will be provided for them, nothing!" At the end, my sister-in-law contacted a private company's funeral vehicle which had departed from Bursa one hour ago, and that driver was kind enough to come all the way back and then transport our loved ones.

There is nothing to say regarding the pain of parents who lost their son and their grandchildren when all words are meaningless but let me continue and tell the story in its entirety.

While traveling in this private funeral vehicle, my poor in-laws were making perhaps the longest trip of their lives. Meanwhile, the news was spreading on Twitter, a deputy in the Parliament and many other people were criticizing the officials in Bursa. In the coming hours, upon the mounting pressure, the mayor would take a step back. Despite knowing that they had already departed Bursa in a private funeral vehicle, the administrator in the municipality who had just a while ago reprimanded my sister-in-law called again and said that a vehicle would now be arranged. They did this because later on, they were going to make a statement like, "We offered to provide them a vehicle, but they didn't accept."

ANGELS OF THE AEGEAN SEA

It was that day when I clearly realized that my belief in God was the most precious treasure I had.

THE LAST FAREWELL

When we arrived to the place where the bodies were going to be washed and prepared for burial, I asked permission from everyone to be the first one to see them. I was in front, and the others behind me as I dragged my feet inside...

This was going to be the last time I would see my husband and my babies in this world, so I wanted to give them a proper farewell. First, I went next to my husband. He was lying peacefully, in a white shroud. I couldn't open his face at first, I just couldn't. My older brother reached over and lifted the cover.

When I saw my husband's face, I just burst into tears. "Oh God! You wanted to take him to Yourself. But I loved him so much, too!" I touched his cheeks, his face, his forehead. He was still so soft despite the three days that had passed. It was as if he was alive, but just sleeping. I kissed his forehead three times. "You left me behind, but please wait for me... please wait until I come to you." Well, I also expressed my disappointment, "I thought you loved me! I thought you loved me even more than our kids! Why did you take them with you and leave me behind?!"

Would you believe me if I told you that I felt like he was alive? It was as if he was going to extend his hands and hug me. That's how real it felt... The people behind me were sobbing uncontrollably as they watched me say goodbye to my husband, again and again. I gave my blessings to him and asked for his blessings.

My son was lying on the bunk under his father. "My dear son!" I said through tears. I touched his hair, his soft face. If we weren't in a funeral home, no one would be able to convince me that they were dead. I would definitely say that they were just sleeping. I kissed and smelled my baby; I inhaled that scent of heaven one last time...

And my daughter... she was lying on another bunk. She looked as if she had gotten taller in the white shroud. She was only eight months old. My baby, my sweetheart. She didn't even get the chance to taste any worldly pleasure. "Come on, wake up!" I said, "Are you hungry? Do you want me to nurse you?" But she didn't open her eyes... I kissed and smelled her many times. This would be the last time I would see my family... in a funeral home in my husband's hometown.

It was that day when I clearly realized that my belief in God was the most precious treasure I had. If I were not a believer, in the face of such a huge pain, I would probably go insane... there would simply be no reason to live anymore.

...

It was very crowded at the funeral. The roads were filled with people who came to say farewell to my husband and children, and without exception, every single person was crying. The imam, without any fear, loudly announced my husband and children as martyrs. We were all witnesses that my husband lived a good life and did many good deeds. I was the witness that my husband had never harmed anybody. Neither did my poor innocent babies.

They buried them in the ground, one by one, before my eyes. First, my husband. Then, in the grave right next to his, they buried my son and my daughter together, side by side. They were leaving me behind and going hand in hand to the Eternity.

In the meantime, I heard someone praying loudly. It was a man sobbing and saying "This is the era of Pharaoh! And we are all so powerless and helpless! You martyrs escaped to Heaven! We are left here!" Everyone had drowned in their tears. I found out later that this man was an imam who was slandered and expelled from his job by a decree-law.

ANGELS OF THE AEGEAN SEA

Illustrated by Rana K.

LIFE, DESPITE EVERYTHING, GOES ON

Due to the court's decision that requires me to submit my signature to the local police station in my hometown once a week to prove that I did not leave the country, I cannot visit my husband's and children's graves very frequently.

It takes 17 hours to travel from my town to that other town where my loved ones are buried, and I can only stay a week there. Every day I am there, I spend the entire time at their graves. It is the only place that makes me feel truly happy and at peace… I know they hear me, so I always talk to them… My husband loved to make jokes, and I share his sense of humor. "When I wore a white wedding dress, you were wearing a black suit. Now I have to wear black while you are covered in white." I tell him smiling…

Yes, my husband and children left me behind. But I feel their presence very close to me. Don't ask me how, since I don't know either, but I just feel them.

My husband and I loved each other dearly. I remember that one day we had a conversation about death. We had promised each other that whoever died first, the other would never marry again. I am keeping my promise, for I have three angels waiting for me on the other side… As long as I live, I am going to remain faithful to their memories.

I had a family, I had a home, I had children who were playing and running around in my house… Now I have neither a family, nor a home, nor children. Should I pity myself, or should I feel the pain of my husband and two children who were forced on this journey and then lost their lives?! Where did we stand in this so-called coup? All those people who oppressed us, who let us lose our jobs and then isolated us… Yes, those people who go to their warm homes every evening to their families. I want them to never forget what they did to us and to tens of thousands of people like us. My husband was a devoted father doing everything he could to take care of his family. There was only one option left for us in this country, and that was to escape! Some people begrudged us our peaceful family life in our own country. May God never let anyone else suffer like this.

And today... I am completing my second degree at a university. I am grateful for my family supports me fully. I hope I get to see the day when we aren't labeled as 'terrorists' so that I can find a job and be helpful to others once again. I live my remaining life without any worldly expectations.

My only hope is that one day we can live happily again,

together as a nation.

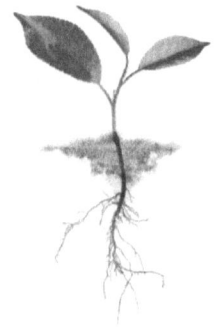

3
FOR GOD'S SAKE, JUST SHOOT ME!

As told by

Birgul Kocal

FOREWORD

The only crime and criminals the young woman ever saw were in movies. Suddenly, she found herself in prison without any evidence of a crime. When she had a severe nervous breakdown because she was unable to bear the separation from her two little children, the head guard in prison threatened her with sending her to a mental hospital. She never shed a tear again.

When she was released pending trial, she found out that her mother was diagnosed with cancer, due to suffering from intense grief. Afterward, she faced the risk of being imprisoned again, in violation of the rule of law. She had no other choice but to leave her beloved country together with her husband and children.

They found freedom in Greece, but new challenges were on the horizon. Unfortunately, she was shocked by her little son's illness.

You will witness the story of Birgül, in her own words who was imprisoned at a young age, left her country by crossing the borders via dangerous routes, and felt the pain of her loved ones.

FORBIDDEN DAISY...

The most prominent thing I remember about that time is that I went into the bathroom, locked the door behind me, and burst into tears... It is weird, I don't remember too much about what happened afterward. I remember sobbing, but I don't remember losing myself completely, punching the walls, scratching my face, and yelling: "I'm not a terrorist! I want to go to my kids!" I pulled myself together hearing the voice of the guards who were trying to open the iron door with a crowbar. I then ran to my ward, went into my bed, and cried some more.

I kept crying until the chief guard came and spoke to me, or rather, threatened me yelling, "If you don't behave, I'll send you to Bakirkoy Psychiatric Hospital! They will drug you there so much that you will not remember your kids anymore, you will even forget who you are!" It was terrifying... I never cried again since I realized I needed to protect my mental health as well as my physical health.

Actually, I did not have much of a nervous breakdown until that day. I had been in prison for one month, but it had felt like a century. I had asked my family not to bring my children on the visit days because I didn't want them to see their mother in prison and like this. My eldest son was seven years old, and my little boy was three. My family was somehow distracting the little one when he was asking about my whereabouts. One and a half months after I was put into prison, I began talking to my elder son on the phone for ten minutes a week. They had told him that I was abroad on a business trip.

Our phone calls were not joyful, neither I was fulfilling my longing. Quite on the contrary, in every single one of them, I was praying for those ten minutes to be over as soon as possible. My son couldn't understand and accept my departure, and he kept pushing me with statements like "Why did you leave without telling me? I have toys and clothes, and I don't want any allowance money, please come back! If you loved me, you'd come back! You may not know how to come back, but you could search Google!" No matter what I said, I couldn't convince my son that I loved him so much.

I was afraid I would forget my children's faces, so I told my parents to find an excuse and bring them. I said, "Explain this place, the soldiers, and my being here with a reasonable story, then bring them." When I told my son on the phone that we were going to meet, he said he wanted to bring his school report card and show it to me, but I told him not to do so. I didn't want him to be upset if the prison guards didn't let him bring it in. As it turns out, my little boy saw a daisy by the sidewalk while he was waiting outside and plucked it to give it to me. But the soldiers took it from him at the entrance and threw it away, and for minutes, he could not stop crying.

We were sitting at a table where we were not even allowed to hug our loved ones. My eldest son jumped on me, saying, "Mommy! Mommy!" My husband, my mother, and my father were not allowed to have physical contact with me, but I took my kids, put them on my lap, and wrapped them in my arms. My eldest son had been told that I was here for a short time and that I had to go abroad again, but he couldn't accept this explanation. "Mommy, do you have to go abroad right away? Please come with us, stay at home at least one night". He was pressing on and saying things like: "If you can't stay with us, I'll stay with you". At one point, he leaned forward and whispered softly in my ear, pointing under the table: "You don't really have to stay here, mom. Hold my hand, let's run away hiding under the tables." What a difficult situation for a mother!

When the visit time was up and they took my sons away from me, I felt like they were ripping my nails off. The bell rang, announcing that the time was up, but I had not been with them long enough yet; I was hugging and kissing my sons again and again. Imagine, you haven't seen your precious ones for a long time, and you won't be able to see and touch them again for at least two more months. I was so miserable. My eldest son desperately shouted, "Mom, please don't go away! I want to take you home!"

That was it, that was the day when I ran and locked myself in that bathroom. That day, all day long, I was grappling with questions inside me that I couldn't answer. I wasn't rebelling against my fate, but I couldn't accept it, either. What kind of security threat could a three-year-old's daisy pose? What have we done to deserve this? Why did my kids have to visit their mother in prison? I couldn't understand it, I couldn't accept it!

...

THE MOST LOYAL SPOUSE IN THE WARD...

I was working as a civil servant at a courthouse. My husband, who was a computer engineer at TUBITAK,[11] was fired from his job without any reason or concrete evidence in May of 2016. Those were the days when we trusted no one and couldn't share our troubles or grief. It wasn't long before we found ourselves in the middle of a social massacre that occurred after the July 15th coup - an event that I only heard about on TV that night, while I was cooking for my guests at home.

It was July 31, 2016, when the police had raided our home in the morning. They searched our house and cars for 3-4 hours and confiscated all the electronic devices. As they were taking my husband away with them, the captain of the officers turned to me with an evil expression on his face and said mockingly, "Say a big goodbye to your husband, because you'll never see him again!" My husband calmly told me: "Don't cry, honey! This is what they want, to hurt us." But I just couldn't stand it, and I cried. Thankfully, my eldest son was with his grandmother, and the little one was asleep.

For the next 16 days, I was working during daytime and waiting in front of the police department in the evenings. I was bringing clothes or personal things for my husband every day. I was not leaving until the police accepted them. I was especially purchasing new clothes so I could write on their labels how much I loved him. Were the officers delivering

---

[11] The Scientific and Technological Research Council of Turkey, a national agency of Turkey whose stated goal is to develop science, technology, and innovation policies.

those items to him? If they did, would he be able to notice my notes? Maybe, I did not know...

What I surely did not know was that during ten days of his sixteen days in custody, my husband was lying on a stone floor with his hands handcuffed except for the need for the toilet...He had lost about 18 pounds in two weeks... The officers piled up the people they had detained and crowded them into such inhuman conditions that after a while, the officers were disturbed by the heavy smell in the air and only then permitted the prisoners to change their clothes. So, the clothes I left for him and the notes I wrote on their labels were eventually delivered to my husband. I later learned that the ward mates of my husband declared me as 'the most loyal wife'. I was writing tiny little notes on cloth labels with care: "Honey, no matter how long it takes, I'll come every day... I love you so much, don't be sad and don't be afraid... I'll always be here for you... We're fine, and we're going to get through it all, as long as you're doing fine over there."

It's hard to be in prison, but it's more difficult to be outside without knowing anything about the situation of your loved one inside... We were hearing about torture news every day, and we were getting worried. We did not know my husband's condition. I was going to learn later that my husband wasn't tortured in prison, but during the nights he heard screams coming from the depths of the building, the screams of those who were being tortured!

I was desperately going to work during the daytime, waiting in front of the police building in the evenings, begging, and praying to God.

It was August 16, 2016, Tuesday. My husband had a court trial that day, but I couldn't get a leave from work because no one at my office knew about our situation. I sent my sister and brother-in-law to the trial and went to work. We were set up with such a cruel trap that day, the police came to my office, confiscated my computer and my bag, and detained me.

...

"I AM FINE; YOU WILL BE FINE AS WELL!"

In the boiling heat of August, 48 people were stuffed into those small wards and we were trying to sleep like building a puzzle. Pregnant women, sick women around, we are all half hungry, half thirsty... During my eleven days in custody, they didn't let us take a shower, there was no air conditioning, either. And we were being mocked by the guards as they constantly told us: "You smell like sheep!"

While in custody, I was begging the police officers to learn about my husband's condition, but I couldn't get an answer. My friends with whom I had been dumped into this hole, like sheep waiting to be sacrificed, were at least having visits from their families who were bringing them their needs. But I was neither getting a call nor were my needs being provided for. I was so upset, and I wondered if my parents were just ignoring me. I wondered if anybody was there for me anymore. That's your biggest fear when you are in prison: "Do they believe I'm guilty? Will my husband abandon me?" But more than that, both when my husband and I were in prison, I worried about one single thing the most. It was, "Will we snitch on someone?" Yes, would we snitch on an innocent person to save ourselves? Of course, we were not planning anything like that, at all. But then again, how could we be sure about ourselves? The conditions in the prison were brutal. People were being tortured horrendously and they were being threatened with harming their family members and their young children.

It was impossible to see daylight in prison. We did not know the time. They even took our statements inside the building, especially at night, to further our psychological stress. When it was 9:00 a.m. and 9:00 p.m., there was a shift change, that was how we were tracking the time and the days.

One day, as we were walking out to be taken to the health clinic for reporting any assault, I saw a package at the police checkpoint. Yes! My name was written on it! Who knew for how many days it was sitting there? I was able to get my package by insisting to the police. The package was from my husband! He was released a few days ago pending trial. There were spare clothes and personal care products inside the package, and just like me, he wrote little notes on the labels. I liked the one on top of the wet wipe box the most: "Honey, I'm fine, you'll be fine as well!"

...

Source: AST International Human Rights Art Contest

DARK CELLS

I was included in a case file involving 130 former court employees like me. On Friday night, August 27th, 2016, in the courtroom on the 11th floor, the imprisonment order was issued for all of us, 30 women and 100 men.

There were rumors that some of the women in prison were being sexually harassed, especially our sisters who belonged to the Hizmet movement. We were all shocked and burst into tears as we listened to one of our sisters we met in prison, who was transferred here from Afyon prison. After arresting and taking away their husbands, ignoble characters attempted to dishonor their wives. So many sisters, and so young, were dumped into solitary confinement cells... Worse than even pharaohs, disgraced and evil characters performed atrocities by shoving our brothers and sisters into cars and taking them to the nearby forest to abuse and torture them. When I heard all that evil, in addition to all these injustices, the lawlessness, and persecution we were already experiencing here, drove me insane. Something must have been done to shout out to the world of what I heard, the human rights abuses of all those who have been persecuted. Our silent cries were rising into the sky with our prayers. We were confused; what should we do, what should our brothers and sisters who have been subjected to these atrocities do? What if I will be one of those tortured?

I have to admit that when I heard the order of imprisonment, my world collapsed on my head. I just wanted to jump out the window and die purely. I asked the lawyer if I could use her phone and then called my sister. We both cried on the phone: "They're throwing us into prison, sis!"

We were despised so much by the public that we were even taken to the hospital through the back door so we wouldn't be attacked by others. Think about it - a handful women who had never harmed anyone in their lives!

...

I don't need to explain how nightmarish our first days in prison were. First, we were put into an incredibly dirty and unlivable temporary ward, then into a cell. We were not allowed to clean around. When we asked for water, they brought a water bottle with a chewed gum stuck on the inside of its lid. We were not allowed to have fresh air; they treated us worse than ISIS prisoners.

The first day we were taken to the wards, we were like fish out of water. There were 13 of us in a two-floor ward, and we were all in jail for the first time; we were rookies here, so to speak. We did not have the slightest idea of what to do or how to do anything. We heard someone shouting "Mess!" and a pot of soup was left under the door. But with no forks, spoons, and plates! "Write a petition and take it on the day of the canteen!" the guards responded. OK, but how were we supposed to eat until the day of the canteen? Please, give us what we need now, and we would pay when our family brings money for us. Finally, with grunts, they gave us only spoons. Ten spoons for thirteen people... we took turns eating.

No soap, no towels, no napkins... In two of the four extremely small shower cabins, there was no running water, and in one of the other two, it was barely tolerable. Pretty much, 13 people were to share one shower cabin. When we asked for something, the answer was always the same: "Write a petition, you'll get it on the day of the canteen!" "Come on, at least give us a pen and a paper to write a petition!" But we had to buy the paper and the pen from the canteen as well. A strange dilemma...

We learned everything by experience. There was an 8:00 a.m. and a 6:00 p.m. count every day, and everyone should be in the front of the ward at those times.... I once was scolded as I was in the shower at that time. After some time, we met with a few experienced prisoners from another ward and learned from them about the rules and regulations around.

...

The first day that we were taken from the cells to the ward was the restricted visit day. My husband and his parents came. My parents couldn't come because they were taking care of our children. I had just gotten out of a cell, and I still couldn't get over being incarcerated and looking at the man I loved only behind a glass. I cried a lot that day...I kept saying: "Don't forget me here! Don't leave me here!" My husband and his family got so sad. "Don't do that Birgül!" my husband begged. "Sweetheart, why should we forget about you? I came every day in front of the police station when you were detained and waited for you."

Human beings get used to everything somehow. So did I. At the next visit, I was smiling at them. But because I had cried so much during the previous visit, they were so stressed this time. This time, it was me who comforted them.

"MINUTES ARE LIKE MONTHS IN PRISON"

A strange place, dungeon... "Father killers and fathers are kept together." as the poet Necip Fazıl Kısakürek[12] states. Innocents are not tolerated as much as the robbers and murderers in prison, and "might surely makes right" in that place of suffering.

We heard crazy screams some nights... "Why on earth does a woman yell like that?" we were discussing. We learned afterwards that her name was Sekibe... We heard her story and were terrified. She had murdered her family and was transported here after staying in a mental health hospital; she was being moved from ward to ward, but no one wanted her... Everyone was talking about her, and we were scared, too. "We hope

---

[12] Necip Fazıl Kısakürek is a Turkish poet, novelist, playwright, and Islamist ideologue.

they will not bring her to our ward!" Thank God, they did not.

Then we heard another voice at night. We listened to her, too. It was not like Sekibe; somehow, it was different. Later I learned the truth about it and grieved. A woman who was a formal member of the judiciary was protecting her mental health by speaking out loud and reciting the Quran so as not to go mad in the solitary confinement cell where she was kept. I reserved for her a separate place in my prayers.

One day, I read it in the newspapers. In their headlines, they were slandering and blaming Hizmet movement members for making plans to escape from prison. I got mad at them, grabbed a paper and pen, and wrote in big letters: "ESCAPE PLAN: first, ablution to be performed, then chapter Fath from Quran to be recited 19 times, all the other prayers to be said, then escape by flying away!" I hid the plan under my bed intentionally so the soldiers could find it when they came to search. But my ward mates got so scared, they begged me not to do this and finally tore the plan apart.

...

Sometimes I had questions in my mind like: "Why am I here? What am I doing here?" Yet sometimes I thought that I was put there by God to witness all the torture and pain around: Women who got sick and fainted because they were not given their blood glucose monitors, women in fever and pain who had recently given birth and were not allowed to breastfeed their babies; those who worked hard for over one month to make toy trains using tea boxes as a holiday gift for their children but even that was considered to be against the prison rules... Those who weep every day in a corner... and all those slanders. I think I had figured out why we were all here: To witness and testify to all this cruelty and injustice in the Hereafter.

When I was stressed, I had a habit of clenching my teeth, since a long time ago. Well, what is more, stressful than being in there? Every day in prison, I clenched my teeth so hard that I soon broke two teeth from the upper right and lower left. They were hurting so much; I could hardly eat by filling the cavities with cotton pieces. Even though I had written petitions many times, I was allowed to see a dentist only after two months. At my first visit, the dentist said that he cannot take care of me because he needed to attend another emergency case, so he left after making a new appointment. Another dentist did such a sloppy and careless filling in one of my teeth, and he didn't even request for me to be uncuffed during this time. As soon as he was done, without looking at me, he told the guards to take me away, as if he was talking about an animal. Only in my third visit, thankfully there was a conscientious dentist. After he told the guards to take off my handcuffs immediately, he did his job in a very polite and meticulous way. He talked to me, asked me about my story. And after he listened to me, he said to comfort me: "Look, where I work is no different than a prison, either", referring to the high-security room in the basement of the hospital, a small room with barred windows. I smiled bitterly at him and said, "I hope these bars remain to be the only bars you stay behind."

MY LITTLE SON

It was August 16th when I was imprisoned. About two months later, I decided my little son to join me in the prison. He was only three years old; he wouldn't realize that we were in prison. I thought I would feel better if he stayed with me for a while. When my family came for an in-person visit, they brought him, and he stayed. But there was one thing we had forgotten. He had a seizure about a year ago, and we had watched him at nights for a week in case he might have another one.

They had allowed me to keep my son, but they wouldn't let me take his medicines or his toys, and after a while, allergic symptoms began to show. His nose was running, and it was often blocked. One night it got worse; he had a fever, and he could barely breathe. He was crying nonstop, and my efforts of dipping a napkin in salty water and dripping it in his nose didn't help. I called the guards many times, but no one came. All night long, my child cried continuously and all the women in the ward watched him helplessly in tears. At that time, there were 23 women in the ward. My child's fever continued for two days. I begged them at least for a nasal spray, but no! I asked them to call my husband to take my son to the hospital. No! Could you at least give me a syringe so I can drip salty water into his nose? They didn't even give me a syringe!

During that time, three faucets of the four shower cabins we shared were not working. The single cabin with a working faucet did not have a shower sprinkle. So, whenever my son had a high temperature, I was washing him in the toilet of the ward. This continued for two weeks, almost every night. That he was staying with me was cheering me up, but after a while, it became torture for both of us.

October 21st... I was washing my son again when I heard people downstairs screaming and yelling. What was going on? When I finished washing my son, I wrapped him up, entrusted him to a friend, and ran downstairs. Eleven of my friends had learned that they would be released soon, they were screaming with joy. I had been arrested on the same charges as them. A friend of mine and I were not to be released. I can't explain in words how upset I was. I couldn't stand my son going through this with me any longer. How could I take care of him when I hardly could take care of myself? A few days later, I delivered my son to his father, shedding tears of blood.

UNEXPECTED NEWS!

During the time I was arrested, my mother had some health problems and was frequently visiting the doctors. When I was in prison, she came a few times at first, but then she didn't show up. I was often told that she couldn't come because she was looking after the kids. I knew, or at least I could guess, that she was very upset with my situation... What I did not know was that every day she desperately hoped and waited for her daughter to come home and then collapsed at the end of each day. I did not know that while waiting in front of the prison on the visiting days, she fainted twice... Once she fell and broke her teeth; the other time, her fingers were injured... And finally, she was diagnosed with bowel cancer.

I had a strong physical health; I was not getting sick quickly. But the same thing could not be said for my mental health. On the contrary, my husband was a psychologically strong man, but he physically fell ill very quickly. If he were to stay in prison, his body wouldn't be able to handle the severe conditions of the prison. And if I were out, I wouldn't be able to handle my children's psychological problems and, especially, my mother's illness. I think God Almighty treats us with mercy, even here.

My husband - may God bless him - never made me feel alone; he always supported me and somehow managed to make me laugh. It was in our destiny to be apart from each other on our 10th wedding anniversary. Since it wasn't a visiting day, we just talked over the phone. He had bought for me a present, and no matter how much I insisted, he didn't tell me what it was, as it was a "surprise." I have to admit I was not too strong emotionally during our conversation on that phone call. I couldn't bear all those things I was living through, and when I told him that, he said something wonderful to me: "Thank God you're innocent, we're innocent... I'm proud of your righteousness. You have been tested in there for your righteousness, and I'm being tested here by desperately looking at my loved one behind bars. Thank God, either way, we're living the lives of saints in these hard times. I hope we will receive the fruit of our actions, sooner or later!"

My husband said he'd bring my wedding anniversary gift on the day of his visit, but I was thinking, "What could he have bought that would be allowed in?" Finally, when he came with my mother, I noticed his hands were empty. It was a restricted visit; I was talking to my mother over the phone behind the glass; my husband suddenly took off his coat and then his jacket. When he started unbuttoning his shirt, I was about to ask my mother: "What's he doing?" But then I saw my present when he took off his shirt and was left with a white t-shirt! For a long time, I had wanted to purchase a bag and a wallet of a brand I really liked. Apparently, my husband bought them for me, took pictures of them, pressed the pictures on a t-shirt, and came to show them to me. I felt on top of the world! Praise be to our Lord, who rejoiced us even in prison.

...

FOR GOD'S SAKE JUST SHOOT ME!

It had been six months since I was imprisoned, and there was no indictment yet. The district attorney's office was constantly deciding to continue my detention despite my objections every month! And when our indictment was finally written and submitted, we were only going to learn about it on TV: "The indictment was filed about the terrorists who had leaked into the Istanbul court system" the news anchorman was saying. How strange! We were ordinary people with routine lives, yet we were being referred to as members of a terrorist organization.

As 130 people were in the case file, we had to be all present in court at the same time, which meant the trial would take days. We were transferred to Silivri prison for the first trial in April. It was like being arrested, all over again. The same ordeal - the pat-down search, the temporary ward, the solitary confinement cells, seizure of our belongings, etc. But they were much more thorough since this was a high-security F-type prison. Even our most private clothes were being revealed. When we went through the x-ray device, we were exposed to a pat-down search and then to a strip search in a room.

It was a nightmare. I had a tunic on me and apparently, there was a tiny piece of an iron label in one of the pockets. They let me pass through the x-ray machine over and over, and when they couldn't figure out why the machine was beeping, they forced me to take off all my clothes in front of the soldiers. I begged them for a female officer to search me in a room. They didn't accept it. I looked, in tears, at the commander of the soldiers who was standing in the corner of the room, and I begged: "For God's sake! For God's sake, shoot me! I can't stand it! Let this ordeal end for all of us! You would say that I was running away, ok? Just shoot me! You've already arrested me as a terrorist!" I was crying my heart out, and my friends were crying, too. Even some guards were upset. Then they took me to the private room.

...

And the court...

The trial took several days. It was sad to see some of the people snitch. But there was also another woman who said: "My husband and I had such a bad relationship that I was afraid he'd kill me. But these women here took care of me. We were praying together, reading Qur'an." The judge who heard this would ask, with his eyes blazing: "Really? What chapters were you reciting in Quran?"

I can't forget the words our lawyer said that day: "Your Honor, you and I have been in these courtrooms for many years. Do you realize this is the first time we are speaking about the chapters of the Quran in this terror court as evidence of a crime, and not about bombs or weapons?"

One of our friends said during her defense that her mother died of diabetes a decade ago, and she herself had advanced diabetes and that it was extremely difficult for her to survive in the prison. I knew her very well, some time ago she was in severe depression because she had been constantly denied the food she was supposed to get, and she tried to commit suicide by eating plenty of chocolate. Something amazing happened the next day when we got to the trial. Apparently, some of the brothers in other wards had learned about her condition earlier. On that day of trial, when they left their wards, they put a few nuts in their pockets. They passed them hand-to-hand in a great deal of solidarity in the courtroom and secretly delivered them to our diabetic friend! They repeated this every court day. While the judges of the court had absolutely no mercy, those who were defending themselves against all sorts of lies and slanders were such a monument of mercy!

After ten days of trial, no decision was issued from the court. One week later, the trial continued, but no decision from that one, either!

...

It was our last court trial in Silivri Prison. When we were brought into the main hall, I saw my husband waving at me. All the detainees were confined into a booth surrounded by soldiers. "The defendants are admitted without handcuffs!" announced one officer. I have to admit, hearing this, I felt like an animal. I thought, "They are handcuffing us to each other when we are taken into and out of the prison, and they are even surrounding us with soldiers. I had a fleeting moment of self-doubt: I don't remember any sort of crime I have committed, but perhaps I committed a crime without realizing it?" There was no other explanation for all the security measures that were not even taken for real terrorists.

They had handcuffed me together with a young woman, she was not married yet. Even in that situation, she joked, whispering: "Well, I had always thought my hand would only be connected to some other hand with an engagement ring." We giggled.

...

It was May 12th. We were finally being transferred from Silivri prison back to Bakirkoy woman prison. Meanwhile, our last trial was in the Caglayan courthouse with the participation of families and lawyers. We did not know the verdict yet, but we had a joyous hope thinking we're going home... The weather was pleasant, we could see out the window. The families of two of our friends were waiting at the entrance gate of the prison, we thought perhaps only those two friends were to be released.

During our time in Silivri, we were never given our right to a phone call. Thus, I had no opportunity to inform my family about the visit on the next day. As soon as we entered Bakirkoy prison, I began to tell the guards: "We have a right to a phone call! We want to use it right now!" Meanwhile, the court decision was expected to arrive at any time. However, I had no hope left for being released, so I kept telling the guards that I wanted to use my phone call right. Then the small slot on the door was opened. By the way, that slot is so low that you need to get down on your knees in order to be able to see anything. I ran to the door and got down on my knees: "Do you let me use my phone call right? Can I call my family!?" The guard looked at me with a cold expression, announced my name and the names of two other of my friends, and said: "Get ready to be released!" Well, I was not expecting this at all. I stood there for a moment, frozen! I was so focused on using my phone call right that I couldn't fully comprehend the meaning of the word 'release'.

My friends in the ward came to me with joy, tried to cheer me up, but I was still frozen. I couldn't even be happy... then, I started to cry. I was released, but my closest friend wasn't, and I felt kind of guilty. I hugged her, crying: "I'm sorry! I'm so sorry; I wish we could leave this place together. I had never prayed for only myself!"

I had prepared a list for myself beforehand and hung it on the side of my bunk bed: 'The list of the items to be taken with me, when released'. A friend of mine had taught me Origami, the Japanese art of paper folding. I had made three birds (because it reminded me of freedom); two of them for my sons and one for me. That bird was like a friend to me, I was talking to it sometimes, saying: "We are both in prison, now. But one day, you'll see, we'll fly out of here like a bird." I took that bird first, then a paper flower I had made for my husband, my diary, and a letter which I wrote to my family... I just took these and left all my clothes behind. My husband had given me a headscarf to surprise me on my birthday. No matter how much my friends insisted, I didn't even take that with me.

When there was a court trial of someone in the ward, the others would dress her up like a bride... On my last trial, a friend of mine had given me one of her scarves that matched my shirt... She insisted so much to take it with me when I was getting ready to be released. I wouldn't know then that I would even carry it with me when I was later to cross the Maritsa River to leave the country.

The guards were banging on the door for me to hurry, but I couldn't leave my friends and go out. I finally went out still crying... Everyone else was smiling, but I was in tears.

My friends kept watching me until I disappeared, they were happy and sad at the same time. I was still feeling guilty because I was leaving them behind. I had watched many others earlier through the iron bars when they were released, and I had felt myself like an animal in a cage. Then in the evening, I would think: "Does she sit on a couch now? Does she hug her child? What is she eating? Did she look at the sky, at the sea?" When you're in prison, you dream of what you miss through your released friends.

Now I was going to do those things I dreamed of, but I wasn't happy. Yes, it was sad to be left behind, but it was even more painful for me to leave my friends behind.

My friends were waving and crying... I was leaving and crying.

...

"Always search for your innermost nature in those you are with, as rose oil imbibes from roses."

Rumi

ALL OF THEM AND NONE OF THEM!

When I was in prison, I started watching the TV show 'Inside'. There were two brothers in the leading roles, and they reminded me of my sons. When they were saying, 'Mom' now and then, I was getting sad and crying. Much later I was going to find out that my family was also watching the same TV show just because they knew I was watching it. My sons even had named themselves after those children in that show and reenacted some scenes together. After I was released, I continued watching that show, knowing that my friends in the prison were watching it, too... But I never sat on the couch while watching it. I knew my friends were still sitting on plastic chairs.

While I was in prison, my husband and children had moved out of the house where we had lived together. All my belongings were moved to my mother-in-law's house, and my husband started working in his father's bakery. My father, my sister, my brother-in-law were all there on that first evening together. My mother-in-law had prepared a lovely dinner table, but I couldn't eat much. Where was my mother? Why wasn't she here? "We'll take you to her." they responded.

We drove to her place in two cars. I walked directly into her room. Who was that woman lying on the bed, at most 90 pounds, with tubes from blood bags dangling under her dress? I could not recognize my mother! I was shocked! This wasn't my mother... My mother was fifty-five when I left; and when I came back after nine months, she looked like eighty-five!

...

There is something called 'post-release depression'. I was having difficulties adapting to normal life, after spending nine months in prison. No matter what time I slept at night, in the morning I was waking up at the count-time in the prison. Often, I opened my eyes, looked around, and wondered: "Where am I? What is this place?"

Yes, there were many challenges in the prison, but as soon as I got out, I had to face many other challenges waiting for me outside. My mother was very sick, and we often ended up in the hospital. My husband was working hard, and my kids were constantly complaining about the way I was handling things around: "But my father didn't do it like that!" they were saying at every opportunity. Two families were living together. I couldn't find anything in the house that I was looking for. I was trying really hard to catch up with everything between the house, kids' schools, shopping, and the hospital, but I could not keep up with anything. Suddenly I had become a mother stuck with parental duties up to her neck, the wife of a man who was way too much overworking, and the daughter of a very sick woman. I couldn't breathe; it was so overwhelming. I was all the above, but at the same time, I felt like I was none of them!

I gained a habit in the midst of all this: I was eating an ice cream every day. Amidst all the hustle and bustle, that was my only luxury. One day my husband was so tired, and he said: "Do you really have to eat ice cream every day?" That day, I didn't. Not long after that, my husband came up to me with his eyes red. He had read some of the notes I had taken while I was in prison. I had written: "I miss my family, the wind, the sea, my children... and shameful to say, but eating ice cream." After I got out, we had found ourselves dealing with so many different problems that I had thought it would be inappropriate to say, "Let's go to the seaside!" so I did not bring it up. My husband was so upset upon reading my notes. That day, he apologized and said, "Please eat ice cream every day." And the next day, when he was taking me to the hospital, he parked the car close to the seaside and said: "Let's walk on the beach for a while." God bless him!

...

WHAT DID YOU DO, MOM?

I was released from prison pending trial. In the midst of all this mess, my court day was coming up, and I was trying not to show around how stressed out I was getting. I just couldn't relax, eat, drink, or sleep properly. The trial of 130 defendants lasted for five days. I attended every trial for those five days. At the end, although the prosecutor requested for our arrest, the judge postponed the trial to a further date and did not order to arrest and send us back to prison.

I didn't have any strength left. I couldn't stand one more single day in prison. My constant stress was affecting everybody else in the family. The children's psychology was impaired, all the family members were constantly living with an anxiety. I was too scared to let my loved ones experience those nightmarish months again. My husband and I made a sudden decision and contacted the human smugglers to cross the border illegally into Greece via the Maritsa River. We were going to be ready in a week and would set off at the end of October.

My father-in-law had two bakery stores in Istanbul - one on the Anatolian side and one on the European side. My husband and father-in-law were working in both stores, in rotation. We were staying in my mother-in-law's house on the European side. Because of my mother's medical treatment, my parents started staying with us as well. So even though we didn't tell my parents-in-law, who lived on the Anatolian side at that time, my parents had learned of our departure plans because we were constantly getting prepared for it when we were at home.

My dear mother was frequently thinking of me despite her severe sickness: "I can't stand to see you in prison behind that glass. Go away from here and be free!" I learned that when she came to visit me in prison, she couldn't get out of bed for days afterward because of her deep grief. I never wanted them to, but my parents witnessed every stage of our Maritsa preparations. We bought water-resistant stuff; I sewed bags to put our money in and kept practicing tying baby sling carrier as fast as possible. My mom was getting so sad when she was seeing all of that. We did our best to hide the preparations from her, as long as we could.

You may have heard of the phrase: "Death is the decree of God... if only we were not separated from our loved ones." It was so difficult to say that last goodbye, especially to my mother. I was trying to stay strong, not to make her cry, not to upset her...but it was hard. My mom was very sick, perhaps this was the last time I was seeing her. Then again, I could die too. I didn't care about my death, as long as my children were safe. They had no other option but following us in this journey. Every goodbye is difficult, but it is much more difficult when there are so many lives at stake. That's why we hugged each other and cried, again and again.

My dear father was going to come to see us off only until a specific place. All my life, I had seen him crying only three times: When he visited me in prison for the first time...when during his last visit he was telling me how he could not take care of my children anymore since my mother had gotten very sick, and he had to take care of her. And finally, when he came to Edirne with us to see us off: "Is this how it was supposed to be? How we would separate from each other? Is this how I would send you off?"

He cried so much...I will not forget those moments for the rest of my life.

We were now standing in the middle of the night, waiting for the smugglers to pick us up. For the first time, we explained the truth to our children. I said: "The place you visited me was a prison." I will not forget my eldest son's eyes opening up big and bewildered: "Mom, what did you do?" I tried to explain that I was innocent, that our government and some people just misunderstood us, and one day they would surely realize that they made a mistake. I continued: "But until then, we have to live in another country. And especially tonight, we need to be very quiet. We are on a journey now; we will cross a river soon and then walk a little bit. We are waiting for our friends here."

Hours later, the smugglers finally picked us up with a car and took us near the riverbank. My husband and one of the smugglers were carrying the boat, and I was bringing the kids and our belongings. When we went down to the river, we were going to find out the air pump was broken. All this time, I realized that my little boy had made no sound. I whispered: "Are you all right?" There was no sound! I asked again: "How are you doing?" He wasn't talking. He raised his thumb and made an "OK" gesture. Since I had told them a few hours ago that they should be really quiet, he didn't say a single word!

...

IF YOU HAD GONE WITHOUT SAYING GOODBYE, I WOULDN'T FORGIVE YOU

We were two families on the road to hope. When one of the smugglers pushed the boat with his foot and quickly ran away, we said "Bismillah" (In the name of God) and set out, but the mishaps started coming one after another. The paddle was broken soon. The boat couldn't carry eleven people. We started to spin and drift around, and to our surprise, we hit the Turkish coast every time. I have to admit I was deeply scared, and when we were dragged by the current from one place to another, at one point, I found myself thinking: "Which one of my children should I save if the boat goes down?" The smuggler on the boat finally grabbed on to the long weeds on the shore, still on the Turkish side, and yelled at us: "Get off quickly!" We were confused; we looked at each other's faces, but the smuggler was not joking: "Get off, or I'll let the boat go" he threatened.

We grabbed our children, climbed up a steep slope, and then started to walk. As we blindly walked through the night, not knowing what to do, we saw a car approaching from a distance and we hid in a cornfield. The car came closer and closer; it stopped right in front of the cornfield. And someone in the car shouted: "Get out of there!" We thought it was the police. I whispered to others: "Don't go out, let's recite Yasin from the Quran and pray!" The person who got out of the car was shouting insistently at us to come out of the cornfield. Finally, when he said in the local dialect "Come on guys, get out!" we understood they were smugglers.

It was as if we were in a horror movie; one of the smugglers was driving the car so fast with all the lights off, not pressing the brakes at all so that the brake lights would not come on… "Hold on!" he yelled on the curves as we turned around them so fast. We must have recited all the prayers we knew that night; we were constantly praying. It was around 3 a.m.; we finally reached a house… We spent the night there; the plan was to try to cross the river again in the morning. But when we woke up, it was raining so heavily that we didn't want to go. We called our parents and asked them to pick us up. We had learned our lesson. Maybe we had to say a proper goodbye to our families, receive their blessings, and only then set off.

As a matter of fact, my parents-in-law had been very upset when we left. We had implied to them that we were going soon, but we had not told tell them when. My father-in-law ended up saying to my husband, "If you had gone without saying goodbye, I would never forgive you." We thought every cloud indeed had a silver lining; we were grateful that we returned home.

…

Illustrated by Banu Kalmaz

SORROWS KNOCK ON MY DOOR

A few days later, we gave it a second try. This time we never walked; the smugglers drove us to the edge of the Maritsa. When we arrived, the boat was already inflated, and we were just told: "Get on the boat and go!" It was four of us, another couple with no children, two other men, and two guides on the boat... The weather was calm and there were no waves. Unlike last time, the Maritsa River showed us her pretty face. Later on, my husband was going to describe that night as "Just like having a boat ride in Venice."

The river was easy to cross, but as soon as we landed, it was hard to walk nonstop for 5-6 hours. When my little boy got tired after a while, my companions carried my bags, and I picked him up and carried him. Next, we took a bus, and without being stopped by police, we arrived in

FOR GOD'S SAKE, JUST SHOOT ME!

Thessaloniki, and eventually in Athens.

As we entered Athens, it was midnight, and we didn't have a chance earlier to look for a place on Airbnb. I collapsed on a bench and cried. But I had to be strong. Shortly after, I wiped my tears, and smiled at my kids: "I have an idea guys, let's make a bed right here using our clothes, how about that?" Fortunately, shortly after, a friend of mine called us and invited us to her house so we didn't have to spend our first night in Greece sleeping on a bench outside.

Not long before, we tried to travel from the island of Crete to Europe, but we were detained in the airport because we did not have visas and necessary papers. In the jail where they took us, there was a menacing crowd of detainees, just like in the movies. Some of them were putting their hands out and waving at us from behind the bars... Some were swearing... some were blowing kisses... I was terrified for a moment that they were going to put us in the same place with them. Thankfully, they placed me in the women's ward with my children. My husband was in the men's ward right next to us. I was used to staying in a jail cell, but it was difficult for my kids. My eldest son kept holding the iron bars and cried, "Why am I in jail? I am just a child." Unfortunately, I couldn't stand it either, and we all cried together.

There was a female cop watching the women's ward. When she asked me why we were here, I told her what we had gone through, pretty much the full story... She couldn't stop her tears. She said, "Enough! Do not tell me anymore! I also have two children. I can't stand it... I wish I could let you get on a plane to Germany right now... I wish I could at least take your kids out from here to a park." She was so sincere and kind-hearted. I apologized to her because we had illegally entered their country. I told her that we had never committed a crime in our lives; we just had to save ourselves and our children… And then, to my surprise, she apologized to me. The reason was, in her words: "You Turks did not destroy our churches in Istanbul, but we destroyed all your mosques here. Please forgive us!"

This Greek police was so kind, she made a huge favor to us. She brought my husband from the other ward and put both of us with our children in a separate cell; she even brought us food. She said that she would come back after ten minutes, but she didn't for one and a half hour not to disturb us. That day I remembered how for years we had been told that Greek people were our enemies. I was so ashamed.

God is so great that even here in this Greek prison, He sent good-hearted people to help us. Tashi from Tibet, Julietta from Cameroon, and Sara from Iran… three beautiful-hearted women of different nationalities… Sara was comforting me saying: "Look, I don't even have a family, but you're on your way to being with your family all the time. Your husband is in the next ward; your kids are with you." Julietta played with my kids and kept them busy. The kids were crying and being cranky on the first day, but they cheered up when they started playing with Julietta. When we went to bed in the evening, I said to my children: "Let's pray. Let us pray that God will send us back to our house with the pomegranate tree in its garden." My son just put his hands down and said: "No, I want to stay here!"

Five days later, we were released. I said goodbye to my good-hearted friends in the ward… Julietta cried behind us until we disappeared.

…

FOR GOD'S SAKE, JUST SHOOT ME!

We had been in Greece for four months. Then, my husband went to Germany, there were not many job opportunities in Greece. I stayed with my children for six more months in Greece, waiting for a family reunion visa. We had a tiny house; a little table in it, at which the three of us were studying. I was attending a German language course and helping my children with math and English. I was making new Greek friends, too. Days were passing, I was feeling really good.

Often, I was going to the German consulate. I was helping to interpret for my friends, using my English. When one of my friends received a visa, we were hugging each other and crying with joy. I spent so much time in the consulate, eventually, the officer working there knew me very well. She promised me that one day soon, she would call me, to give me good news about my visa.

Then, on February 13, 2018, my husband was interviewed for residency in Germany. He said that the interviewer was very strict, and he didn't think it went so well. He called again shortly, this time he was crying because he had heard the story of the Abdurrezzak family, who had died while trying to cross the Maritsa River on a boat. We had met them in Turkey, and they were the nicest people. I couldn't believe it; I cried so much...

The sad news was coming after one another. Not too much time had passed after we had learned about the Abdurrezzak family when we received another bad news about the death of our beloved sister Esma (Esma Uludag) who had fled to Greece from the persecution in Turkey. Our families were so close, our children were good friends with each other. I was deeply shaken by both of these very sad news that we had received back-to-back. Until I had heard about these news, I was trying to be positive and socially involved, learning German with enthusiasm. Suddenly I turned into a sad and desperate woman...

EID[13] IS JOY TO MANY, BUT SORROW TO ME...

The Eid was coming up, and there was good news from my husband. We would have a family reunion soon in Germany. Meanwhile, my little boy (five years old) was getting unexplained purple bruises on his body. I was thinking: "I don't have any official documents; there's no way I can take him to a hospital here, it is best to go to Germany as soon as possible and take him to a doctor there."

But one night all of a sudden, my son had a fever. I watched over him until morning; there were so many bruises on his body. I was not able to do anything to help him. I was desperately crying. That morning I called a doctor who himself was also a refugee like us and took my son to him.

It was Eid Eve. The doctor examined my son quickly and said: "You can leave your elder son here; I will take care of him. You have to take this kid to the hospital immediately. My wife will accompany you." I didn't make too much sense of it, but I did what he said. Later I figured out why his wife was to accompany me to the hospital. Because of the disease that he suspected, his wife was with me to support me when I hear the unexpected news so that I would not be left alone.

We took my son to the hospital, they ran tests immediately, and we waited. Meanwhile, my husband called. He was so happy, he was looking for a house, we were soon to reunite. When I told him that we were in the hospital, he was still calm. He said: "Don't worry, hopefully, it is not

---

13 A religious holiday celebrated by Muslims.

something serious."

The next morning it was Eid holiday. I was praying "God, please give us good news on this holy day. Please!" Test results came out late in the evening, and they were not good at all. The doctor said that he suspected leukemiaI simply collapsed!

...

During the last two Eids, I was either in prison or in the hospital taking care of my mother. When we were making plans to leave Turkey, I was hoping that I could finally have a happy Eid with my family together. Alas! Today was the Eid celebration, I was again in a hospital.

I had promised my kids I'd buy toys for them on Eid day and take them to the playground. Here I was, crying in a hospital hallway. Meanwhile, my husband called again. I gave him the sad news, and we cried together over the phone. Soon after, the doctor came and said that leukemia had already infected 89% of the platelets in my son's blood. They wanted to start chemotherapy immediately, and I had to give my consent for it by signing a consent form.

It was early in the morning; I ran straight to the German consulate. I was begging the officers: "Please give us an emergency travel certificate!" They said there was no way that they could give us anything until my husband's documents arrived from Germany. Meanwhile, the hospital was asking for an emergency signature to start the chemotherapy immediately. It was such a tense moment. I called my husband and said: "It's very risky that we get on a plane. Even hours are important for our son right now... we are staying here!"

It was so difficult... But God was not leaving us alone and helpless in this country where we were just refugees. So many people, especially Hizmet volunteers, prayed for us and supported us. People, who were refugees themselves, brought us food and clothes. Even people we didn't know rushed to support us when our story was in a Greek newspaper. I especially remember a Greek woman who was living in Istanbul earlier and was harassed and expelled from Turkey just because she was a "non-Muslim." She said: "You are expelled, too, just like me." And then hugged me in tears. My son had been asking for a Spider-Man t-shirt for the last two days, and when we opened the package she brought for us, lo and behold, there it was: A Spider-Man tracksuit and a Spider-Man cup! My Lord responded to my son's prayer through the good heart of this Greek woman. We shed tears of joy and gratitude.

After sister Esma had passed away, I just couldn't pull myself together. I was so impatient to leave Greece to reunite our family in Germany. But now, after everything that happened, I realized that I should have asked God by saying: "Give us what is best for us!"

Two weeks later, the visa proceedings were cleared, and my husband was given a travel document. He flew right to Greece. We stayed together for a week, and we were told by the doctors that our son could travel. The day we would get on the plane, my son was going to get a blood transfusion here, and as soon as we landed in Germany, he was going to be taken to the hospital. I had been waiting for this moment for so long, but I wasn't even able to experience that joy and excitement because of my son's illness. My only wish was for my son to be healthy again.

...

FROM SECOND HOMELAND TO THE THIRD...

Our second homeland was Greece... Then we came here, our third destination: Germany... The first eight months here passed with intensive treatment of my son. He will continue to be treated for two more years, but he can now attend his school. The days when he had lost his hair and eyebrows are gone, thank God.

After three nightmarish years, I finally live-in peace. We have a home, and my son is recovering. I have no fear of being arrested by police. Even though I'm far away from my mother, I can talk to her over the phone. What else can I ask for? Alhamdulillah (Praise be to God)!

I don't consider going back to Turkey at all. When we had left Turkey and arrived in Athens, I was full of anger. I am calm now, but I will be resentful forever... I don't miss anyone but my family. I didn't cut all the bonds with my country, but I've disconnected from people who deemed all those sufferings proper for us.

I hope to spend more time with my children and make up for the days that we couldn't be together. My only worry is about my son's complete recovery. All these events have taught me not to make big plans for the future. Now I say, "I have no dream but health for myself and my family. But I have great dreams for humanity, for Hizmet Movement."

I had spent the last three religious festivals either in prison or in the hospital. When I got here, I made a decision: I wasn't going to celebrate any upcoming festival until all my brothers and sisters in prison could celebrate it together with their families! But I changed my mind when I was advised that this would be unfair to my children. We've had some lovely religious festivals since we got here, thank God! At least I made it to the playgrounds with my kids.

My husband was able to get a job in his profession one year ago; he is working full-time now. I've improved my German a lot; I take my son to hospital appointments, attend his school parent-teacher conferences. I've been accepted to join a local government project for immigrant women, they're helping me to fulfill my dreams. I got admitted into Bochum University. I think I have a talent for languages. I want to work as an interpreter in the future, when I finish college.

I still have the forgetfulness from my days in prison. I had prayed so much in those days, I was saying: "My Dear God, please make me forget the names of all my brothers and sisters who belong to the Hizmet Movement! So that even if I am tortured in this jail, I would not betray them, and I would not be able to remember their names, even if I wanted to. Please let me forget their names."

I still keep forgetting things in my daily life.

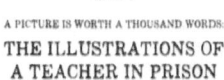

www.ingramcontent.com/pod-product-compliance
Lightning Source LLC
Chambersburg PA
CBHW031414210526
45464CB00005B/1876